White Cliffs Media Company

Performance in World Music Series

Lawrence Aynesmith, Series Editor

- *Salsa!: The Rhythm of Latin Music.*
  Charley Gerard with Marty Sheller.

- *The Music of Santería:*
  Traditional Rhythms of the Batá Drums.
  John Amira and Steven Cornelius.

- *The Drums of Vodou.*
  Lois Wilcken, featuring Frisner Augustin.

- *Drum Gahu: The Rhythms of West African Drumming.*
  David Locke.

- *Drum Damba: Talking Drum Lessons.*
  David Locke, featuring Abubakari Lunna.

- *Kpegisu: A War Drum of the Ewe.*
  David Locke, featuring Godwin Agbeli.

- *Xylophone Music from Ghana.*
  Trevor Wiggins and Joseph Kobom.

- *Synagogue Song in America.*
  Joseph A. Levine.

SALSA!

S A L S A !

The Rhythm of Latin Music

Charley Gerard

with

Marty Sheller

White Cliffs Media Company
Tempe, AZ

White Cliffs Media Company
P.O. Box 433
Tempe, AZ 85280
602-921-8039

Distributed to the book trade by
The Talman Company
131 Spring Street, Suite 201E-N
New York, NY 10012
212-431-7175

Library of Congress Catalog Number: 88–17164

Printed in the United States of America

Printing number
10 9 8 7 6 5 4

Library of Congress Cataloging in Publication Data

Gerard, Charley, 1950–
    Salsa!: the rhythm of Latin music / Charley Gerard
    with Marty Sheller.
    p. cm. —(Performance in World Music Series; no. 3)
    Bibliography: p.
    Includes index.
    1. Salsa music—History and criticism. I. Sheller, Marty.
    II. Title. III. Series
ML3475.G47 1988   784.5'009729—dc19   88–17164
    ISBN 0-941677-11-7
    ISBN 0-941677-09-5 (pbk.)

Contents

List of Musical Examples

Acknowledgments

I owe thanks to several individuals for their help in bringing this project to fruition. Above all, I wish to thank Marty Sheller. In addition to being my main source of information, he helped rewrite sections of the book pertaining to salsa arranging, and contributed a complete annotated arrangement.

Next, I wish to thank my other sources: John Amira, Frankie Malabe and Oscar Hernández. A significant portion of the book is based on interviews I had with these musicians which were taped and transcribed. The bulk of the interviews took place during Spring, 1988, although interviews with Sheller began in 1984.

Other individuals I wish to thank include: Philip Schuyler, my academic advisor at Columbia University who supervised my research into salsa in 1984; Ramon Rodriguez of Boy's Harbor for giving me access to a large body of material on salsa; Dr. Donald Sherak for lending me his collection of out-of-print recordings; and Evan Sarzin, Esq. for legal advice. I thank Max Salazar, Eddie Bobè and John Amira for reading various drafts of the manuscript.

Special thanks are due to Judith Cook Tucker for taking the time to steer the proposal for this book towards White Cliffs Media Company, and to my editor, Larry Smith, for his invaluable comments.

Lastly, I would like to thank my wife, Dr. Judith Weinstock, and my two children for putting up with me during the writing of this book.

Charley Gerard
New York, 1989

Preface

Insiders and Outsiders

Salsa first caught my attention when I was growing up in the sub-urbs of New York City. Being an avid listener of jazz radio programs, I became acquainted with recordings of jazz greats such as Dizzy Gillespie playing with Latin musicians. Whenever I drove through New York I tuned into the Latin programs on the radio. But even though I enjoyed the music, I often had the feeling I was intruding into someone else's neighborhood.

In 1977 my wife and I moved to Tampico, a gulf coast Mexican city about a five hour drive south of the Texas border. We lived there for almost two years. As a saxophonist, I had always wanted to play in a salsa group. Almost as soon as we arrived, I joined a conjunto ("com-bo") led by a talented local recording artist named Irving Flores.

The repertoire for Irving Flores y su Grupo ("Irving Flores and his Group") was a potpourri, a reflection of Mexico's varied musical tas-tes. We played American rock 'n' roll of the 1950s, mariachi songs, and "música tropical," their specialty. "Música tropical" is the Mexican term for Latin American dance rhythms. Flores' group was a salsa-cumbia band. The cumbia is a Columbian rhythm which is very popular in Mexico. We played salsa-inflected cumbias and cumbia-in-flected salsa songs. As a result, I gained an acquaintance with the salsa repertoire and the rhythms.

After I returned to the United States, I played for a short time with a salsa band in New York. Then for several years my primary relation with the music was as a listener.

Methods for Learning and Research

While undertaking graduate studies in ethnomusicology in New York, I became more and more interested in salsa. I wanted to find out how the music was put together. The few sources on the music which gave musical examples seemed to be outdated or incorrect. I had read enough to learn that the rhythmic formula known as clave was at the heart of salsa. I struggled to pick out the claves, the two sticks that play the pattern. At times I could pick out the pattern, but I often had the feeling that I was imagining it. Other times, I decided that the pattern either was not being played or was not recorded clearly enough on records.

One day I happened to read a review of a Willie Colon record in which an arranger named Marty Sheller was singled out for praise. I decided to get his phone number and give him a call. Although my motivation was simply to find out about the clave and any other aspects of the music, I decided the best approach would be to ask Sheller for salsa arranging lessons. Here was a musician whose knowledge was based on solid experience with salsa, someone whose views I could assume were accurate and up-to-date. I was, of course, cognizant of the fact that Sheller was not Hispanic. I guessed—correctly—that he was someone whose initial contact with Latin music had been as an outsider. Because of this experience, I thought he might be the perfect teacher for another outsider.

Sheller had never taught salsa arranging, so in most respects I directed my own learning experience. To begin with, he showed me how I could tell what the clave was by listening to various unvarying percussion patterns that were nearly ubiquitous. These were played by the cowbell and the timbales. We listened to recordings I brought, and he pointed out the clave. Sheller gave me cassette recordings of songwriters' material which he had arranged. Using these, I wrote my own arrangements for Sheller to evaluate and critique. Again, my intent was not to become a salsa arranger, but to use these lessons to learn about the music. Finally, I showed him instruction books for Latin percussion and various writings on Latin music to see whether he agreed or disagreed with the validity of the musical transcriptions and the assertions made by the authors.

Several years later, when Sheller and I began to plan this book, I selected three other musicians to interview and/or study with to add to my understanding of the music and to add different points of view.

These musicians were: John Amira, Oscar Hernández and Frankie Malabe. In the process of these interviews, the scope of the book was enlarged to include other Afro-Cuban genres and derivative forms as played in New York, as well as their nascence and development in Cuba.

Amira is a percussionist and teacher who plays for Haitian and Cuban religious ceremonies. He is primarily a folklore specialist, rather than a band drummer, and he has played alongside well-known percussionists such as Julio Collazo. Like Sheller, he originally came to Latin music as an outsider from another culture. But in Amira's case, the music was all around him in his neighborhood, the South Bronx. In fact, Malabe also grew up there, and they met over twenty years ago. Malabe and Amira both learned from Arsenio Rodriguez' half brothers, the percussionists Raul and Quique Travieso.

As a teacher, Amira demonstrates an understanding of the African roots of Latin music and culture based on years of transcribing records and studying books on anthropology. He told me that as a result, he probably has gained a more analytic perspective than someone who grew up with the music and culture and who tends to take them for granted. He can quickly express what he plays for a particular rhythm both in terms of rhythmic notation and hand coordination. Nevertheless, he is quick to point out the limitations of information gained from books:

> A book can give notation that may prime you to set about find-
> ing out what the reality of it is. But until you get some real ex-
> amples of it, and listen to it constantly, and try playing along
> with them, or meet people who are capable of playing that way,
> and working with them, it's sort of pointless. It's got to be ex-
> perienced.

We began with lessons on the conga drum. At some point, the lessons turned entirely into interview sessions. As in the interviews I arranged with the other musicians, these sessions were based on questions about various recordings I arranged on a cassette I called "Salsa Examples." I chose each selection for some of the following reasons: to find out the instruments played on a selection; to judge my ability to recognize a folkloric rhythm; to elicit a reaction to deviations from the interviewee's conception of the correct manner of playing. I transcribed all the interviews and showed the transcripts to the interviewees shortly after each meeting. At times I asked one musician to comment on what another said, and showed them the transcripts (which included music notation in addition to text). All the interviews were in English.

Frankie Malabe is a well-known conga drummer in salsa, and is currently active as a teacher. Malabe and Sheller met when both of them were starting out in music. Sheller credits Malabe for teaching him about Latin music, while Malabe credits Sheller with teaching him about jazz. Malabe was the conga player on Pacheco's album, "El Artista," and has worked with the top names in Latin music such as Tito Rodriguez, Tito Puente's rival to the throne of Latin music in the 1950s. Besides playing in bands, he also plays in folklore groups. In this context, he often performs in groups led by Luis Bauzo. Like Amira, Malabe is aware of the literature on Afro-Cuban music, and I was able to elicit information from him by referring to it. Malabe is a Puerto Rican born in New York, what some call Nuyorican (also Neoyorican). He constantly made me realize that Nuyoricans are outsiders to Afro-Cuban folklore, particularly to the religious music, and often get their information second-hand from books and recordings:

> It's hard to get information from the players who are looked upon as the great players in this religious music. For us—Puerto Ricans born in New York or in Puerto Rico—any information we can get is great for us. A lot of the good players have gotten a lot of good stuff from [Cuban anthropologist] Fernando Ortiz' books.

I was referred to pianist and arranger Oscar Hernández by Marty Sheller. I needed a pianist to explain and give me examples of the guajeo, a vamp often used as a powerful rhythmic accompaniment to call-and-response interchanges between the lead singer and the coro ("chorus") and for instrumental solos. Hernández has recorded and performed with Ray Barretto and Ruben Blades, among others. Hernández, a Nuyorican, has a firm grasp of Latin piano and jazz and is classically trained. When I went to his apartment, the piano rack was covered with classical etudes. Hernández is also an arranger who has arranged for several prominent salsa groups and artists such as Típica 73, Barretto and Blades.

While Sheller, Amira and Malabe are all in their forties, Hernández was just thirty-three at the time of our first meeting. His first musical influences were musicians like Eddie Palmieri; his introduction to Cuban artists came after he was already a young performing pianist.

Unlike the others, he seemed comfortable using the term salsa, rather than saying Latin music.

Affiliations and Motives

Myriad levels of affiliations exist for these four individuals because of their backgrounds and musical tastes. Their upbringing in the multiethnic environment of New York City was a very significant factor. Malabe performs both Puerto-Rican and Afro-Cuban folkloric musical genres; Amira, both Haitian and Afro-Cuban. Sheller, Hernández and Malabe have performed with jazz groups. At times they find themselves in the position of an outsider; at other times, as an insider.

Sheller, who is not a fluent speaker of Spanish, is an insider because he has arranged for nearly all the top names in salsa; he is an outsider because the music makes reference to a lifestyle and culture to which he does not belong. Malabe's background as a Nuyorican who learned the music by hanging out on the streets of the South Bronx gives him an "in" into the music. On the other hand, he finds himself an outsider because of the fact that the musical genres he plays are based on the traditions of Cuba, an island with a culture based on different historical circumstances than his own ancestral island, Puerto Rico.

The fact that both myself and the people with whom I interviewed and studied recognized varying degrees of affinities with many different musical communities provided the basis for my approach. It was easy for everyone concerned to slip in and out of roles and to see various topics from different angles. During my research for this book I was, by turns, a fellow musician and teacher, a researcher with anthropological leanings, a fellow student of the literature on Afro-Cuban music, and the author of a book who assigned to others the role of "informant." I was at different times an insider, a participant-observer, and an armchair researcher, delving into the appropriate literature.

Varying my role and even telling the person I was interviewing which role I was assuming at a particular moment proved to be beneficial. Although I might have assumed any of these "roles" when I thought it would unravel some piece of information, they were all sincere. I began my study of the music in the role of a student, in order to find out for myself how the music was put together. This book is the documentation of how I have come to understand salsa and Afro-Cuban music, and how I hope to share that knowledge with others.

PART I

La Música Salsa

Chapter One

La Música Salsa

S alsa is the currently favored name for a form of music, formerly known simply as "Latin music," which has its roots in Cuban popular and folkloric music and is enhanced by jazz textures. The name, which literally means "sauce," became widespread in the late 1960s.[1]

As a music label, salsa has never entirely replaced the term "Latin music." Most musicians, particularly older ones, still prefer the older term. In posters from the late 1960s and early 1970s, the terms are used together. For example, one poster advertises "A New *Salsa* Music TV Show featuring the Top *Latin* Stars"[2] (italics added). The name salsa has recently been accepted in Cuba as "salsa cubana."[3]

Salsa was not the name of a dance rhythm or of a musical genre before this time. It had been used in a musical context before, however. Songwriter Ignacio Piñeiro (1888–1969) wrote a song entitled "Echale salsita" in the 1920s. In addition, the term was used by dancers to urge the musicians to add more indigenous spice to the music, in reference to the spicy sauces used in Latin cooking.[4]

Salsa is best distinguished from earlier styles in Latin music by defining it as the New York Sound, developed primarily by Puerto Rican New Yorkers, known as Nuyoricans or Neoyoricans. The genesis of the music reflects several sometimes contradictory attitudes: a desire to forge roots in Cuban music, an interest in adopting the musical lexicons of jazz and rock, and an often politically-motivated wish to create a pan-Latin American music.

3

National and Ethnic Influences

The Cuban Connection

Many salsa musicians, particularly in the late 1960s and early 1970s, had an atavistic desire to base their music on that of Cuban masters popular in the 1940s such as Arsenio Rodriguez and pianist Lily Martínez Griñan. The adjective "típica" is often used to describe music of this sort. Some Nuyorican musicians who were established in the preceding generation, such as Tito Puente, are still surprised at the new-found popularity of the older style:

> I don't know what's happening now; a lot of the bands are
> sounding like the old bands used to sound when I had my con-
> junto [small group or "combo"]. But they tell me they love that
> sound. Machito and I, we were trying to expand our music,
> make it more progressive.[5]

Many Nuyorican musicians, such as Jerry Gonzalez, who plays both trumpet and conga with equal virtuosity, went back to the roots of the típica sound—to the folkloric music of Afro-Cuba. In the recordings of his band, called The Fort Apache Band (Fort Apache is a name given to a police station in the Bronx), Cuban folkloric music such as comparsa, rumba and the Yoruba chants used in Santería (see Chapter V) are combined with jazz.

The private record collections of bassist Andy González, who is Jerry González' brother, and record producer-musicologist René Lopez were an important source for several of the most well-known musicians on the scene, such as Oscar Hernández.[6] At times, the objective was to duplicate the music, and adopt the musical practices learned from hearing the records. The feeling was that the Cuban way of playing was not only the correct way, but the only way.

The music of salsa musicians often came from contemporary recordings made in Cuba as well as old collectors items. Current recordings were at first difficult to get, but many musicians went out of their way to get them via Martinique.[7] It is now possible to buy them from several sources in the United States.

Due to the isolation of Cuba from the rest of the Western Hemisphere, New York essentially became the new center of Cuban music.

Nevertheless, as in the past, the new trends and dances developed in Cuba after the Cuban Revolution were quickly adopted by Nuyoricans. Before the revolution, musicians picked up the dance rhythms of the mambo, the cha cha and the pachanga, and the descarga, a jam session in the Latin music vein. After the revolution, there was the mozambique and, the most influential new Cuban style of recent years, the songo. It is significant that, despite the break in contact between Cuba and the United States from Castro's rise to power until the Mariel boat lift, Cuba has remained the source of rhythmic innovations. The only new rhythmic developments in the United States involving Latin rhythms have come from outside of salsa. These developments include Latin jazz, Dizzy Gillespie's Cubop (Cuban bop), bugalú and Latin rock—the music of Carlos Santana. All were the by-products of Latin rhythms combined with American popular music styles and jazz.

Although the majority of salsa musicians in New York are Nuyoricans, there have always been a number of Cuban musicians on the scene, most of whom left after Castro's rise to power. First and foremost is Celia Cruz, who possesses a strong, vibrato-less contralto voice and a theatrical flair. She was already well-known in Cuba before she left Cuba in 1960 and resettled in New York. Since then, she has recorded albums with Tito Puente, Willie Colon, Johnny Pacheco and other top names in salsa. Other Cuban musicians who joined the salsa scene include the percussionists Julio (also known as Julito) Collazo, Carlos "Patato" Valdez, Orestes Vilató, Mario "Papaíto" Muñoz, Virgilio and Eloy Martí, Ignacio Berroa and Daniel Ponce; the pianists Javier Vásquez, Alfredo Valdez and Lino Frías; trumpet players "Chocolate" Armenteros and "El Negro" Vivar; bassist Israel "Cachao" Lopez; violinist Alfredo de la Fe and singers Miguel Quintana, Justo Betancourt and Felo Barrios.[8]

Salsa musicians have come from other parts of Latin America besides Puerto Rico and Cuba. For example, Johnny Pacheco hails from the Dominican Republic; pianists Edy Martínez and the late Jorge Dalto are Columbian; Ruben Blades and Mauricio Smith are Panamanian. A handful of non-Hispanic North Americans have made a name for themselves. The most famous is Larry Harlow, born Lawrence Ira Kahn. Other well-known salsa musicians who are not of Hispanic descent include trombonists Barry Rogers and Voirabh Lewis Kahn (who doubles on violin), flutist Art Webb and saxophonists Ronnie Cuber and Bobby Porcelli.

Cuban Perspectives on Salsa

Salsa musicians who are Nuyoricans have occasionally run against the ethnocentrism of Cubans living in the United States as well as in Cuba. Cuban-born Mongo Santamaria is particularly critical of some Nuyoricans who perform Cuban folkloric music, and suggests that, since it is Cuban music, it is best performed by Cuban musicians who have learned it at its source:

> You can't learn to play things like guaguancó here. You have to have been where it came from to know that you kill or get killed for women . . . and drums . . . You can't listen to records and get those feelings.[9]

To balance the record, it must be stated that Santamaria has included several Nuyorican percussionists in his bands for many years. Sheller adds:

> Mongo has always chosen his band members according to their ability to play a variety of grooves including Afro-Cuban music, jazz, funk, samba and soca [soul-calypso]. His band always sounds best when the musicians come from a jazz background and learn from Mongo how to phrase Latin music.

Like Santamaria, Daniel Ponce is a conga player who came from Cuba. Unlike Santamaria, who has been in the United States for decades, Ponce came to the United States only recently, with the group of Cubans on the Mariel Boatlift. Among the Hispanic population, the people in this group are called Marielitos, to distinguish them from earlier waves of Cuban immigrants. Other musicians in this group include jazz alto saxophone star Paquito D'Rivera and drummer Ignacio Berroa. Ponce feels that current popular Cuban music is "absolutely superior" to salsa:

> When the Cubans arrived in New York, they all said 'Yuk! This is old music.' I was expecting to find a stronger Latin scene here; the lyrics, the composition, the feeling are not adventurous. Listen to 1960 Tito Puente or Machito and then listen today. It's different names, but the music and the feelings and arrangements aren't changed. It's a good sound and they're masters, but right now it's necessary for the new generation to make a new sound.[10]

This attitude to salsa on the part of the younger generation of Cubans seems to be widespread. Because of the severance in relations between Cuba and the United States, for many years New York salsa bands had not performed in Cuba. When the Fania All-Stars became the first salsa band to perform there, they were greeted by a lackluster response. After ten or fifteen minutes, the crowd walked out.

There are some indications that attitudes are changing in Cuba, or perhaps the work of some salsa artists is more to the liking of Cuban tastes than others. The popular Cuban group, Los Van Van, recently recorded an arrangement of a song by Ruben Blades. In addition, Richard Egües recorded a song—uncredited on the album—by the Puerto Rican percussionist Angel "Cachete" Maldonado, leader of the group Batacumbele.

The Puerto Rican Connection

It is ironic that in a music dominated by Nuyorican and Puerto Rican musicians, the use of the folk music of Puerto Rico has never been very popular. According to Frankie Malabe, "in live performances you might get one or two merengues in a salsa band. You'll rarely get any bombas and plenas." Bomba and plena are Puerto Rican folkloric forms; the merengue is the national dance rhythm of the Dominican Republic. The Puerto Rican típica sound reached its zenith in popularity among New Yorkers in 1957, when Cortijo performed for large, enthusiastic crowds.[11] It seems that by the 1980s, this sound was regarded as outdated, an opinion which Malabe does not share:

> There are a few of us who still stick to our guns as far as being Puerto Rican. One person who I respect a lot in that sense is Hector LaVoe. He uses the typical vocal phrasing of Puerto Rico. I like playing bombas and plenas. I do them in a folklore group with Luis Bauzo. A lot of guys say, "We don't play that old-hat stuff." That attitude annoys me.

LaVoe was in Willie Colon's band for nearly a decade, a period in which Colon received attention for reintroducing bomba, plena, and other examples of Puerto Rican folklore to the salsa audience.

The American Connection

The young musicians of the new salsa movement wanted to use musical genres associated with non-Hispanic inner-city Americans, par-

ticularly jazz and rhythm 'n' blues. Several of the musicians associated with salsa were previously involved in the bugalú style,
which used Latin instruments, sometimes with the trap set, in creating
a rhythm sounding more like rhythm 'n' blues than Latin music. Joe
Cuba's "Bang Bang" began the Latin bugalú craze in 1966.[13] The style
was an outgrowth of a Black American style known as boogaloo which
was popular in the mid–1960s.[14] Most of the bugalú songs were in
English, reflecting the fact that the young generation of Nuyoricans
were bilingual.

The songs of the bugalú artists reached a national audience, making
big stars out of Johnny Colon, Joe Bataan, Joe Cuba and others. Some
of these bands performed the older Latin dance rhythms in Spanish
along with their bugalú material. The bugalú lost steam by the late
1960s, and the bands returned to an all-Latin repertoire using Spanish
lyrics. (A recent album by Ruben Blades in English is one of the few
substantial exceptions.)

Nevertheless, the influence of non-Hispanic music and the hope of
attracting an audience outside of El Barrio, the Spanish neighbor-
hood/ghetto in New York City, continues to hold sway. In terms of instrumentation, the electric bass of soul music and rock soon took over
the bass spot in the salsa scene. Sheller believes that Eddie "Gua Gua"
Rivera was the first electric bassist in salsa. Perhaps one of the most
popular electric bassists on the recording scene is Sal Cuevas, who
sometimes plays in a funk style.

From jazz came a harmonic vocabulary based on extended harmonies of altered and unaltered ninths, elevenths and thirteenths, as
well as quartal harmony—chords built on fourths. These harmonic
devices first entered salsa in the piano styles of Eddie Palmieri and the
Puerto Rican Papo Lucca. They would take traditional piano figures
based on simple tonic-dominant harmony and elaborate them with
modern harmonies. In the following phrase, older-style pianists
would probably play in octaves with an occasional tenth:

Ex. 1.1. *Piano phrase in octaves.*

Oscar Hernández harmonizes this melody with dominant 7th chords with ninths and thirteenths added:

Ex. 1.2. *Piano phrase with jazz harmonization.*

These modern harmonies are now a staple of salsa arrangers such as Marty Sheller and Oscar Hernández. Although salsa songwriters continue to write melodies consisting of little more than tonic, subdominant and dominant chords, the arrangers enrich the chords, by adding other intervals. In addition, salsa arrangers adopted a melodic style replete with bebop phrases and an occasional quotation from a jazz standard. For example, Sheller put a phrase from the Sonny Rollins tune, "St. Thomas," in an arrangement for Luis "Perico" Ortiz. These forays into jazz have not been universally accepted, since there are many listeners who still prefer the "purer" style of earlier generations. Trumpet player Luis Berrios Serralta, a member of one of Arsenio Rodriguez' bands, believes that the jazz harmonies and jazz phrases are stylistically incompatible with the music. He considers the music to be nothing but badly played Cuban music.[14]

The Brazilian Connection

Some of the leading salsa musicians have an affinity not only for the aforementioned Puerto Rican, Cuban and Dominican dance rhythms, but also for Brazilian music. Willie Colon and Ruben Blades, another former member of Colon's band, are well-known for their inclusion of Brazilian rhythms and, in the case of Colon, adaptations of Brazilian songs. These artists include a short list of Caribbean and South American dance rhythms on a single album, and possibly a rock guitar, funk bass line, or a synthesizer thrown in, depending upon the song. The entire song may be arranged with one rhythm from an area in Latin America. Alternatively, a song may begin, say, as a Cuban mambo, shift to a Puerto Rican bomba and then conclude with a return to the mambo rhythm or even a Brazilian samba. At times, the artists use specialists in the various rhythms, or they are performed by musicians whose primary area of experience is salsa.

The interest in using a wide range of rhythms and even combining them came about only in part for musical reasons. There was a political motive as well. The songs spoke about Latin pride and identity, and the struggle of Latin people everywhere to rise above poverty and persecution. The artists sought to make salsa a pan-Latin American and Hispanic expression. To this "outsider," a subliminal message comes across: "These are all our rhythms, regardless of their local origin. Just as we can combine these rhythms together and rise above their differences, we can rise above the regional differences and become One People."

The Salsa Music Industry

Although salsa can be correctly described as a distinct style (the New York Sound) it must also be recognized for what it is—a creation of the New York commercial music industry. The music reflects the fact that it came into being through the modern technology of the recording studio. Several of the most successful bandleaders are noted for their ability to create their own sound image using the tools of the recording studio, and for choosing the right arrangers and musicians for individual spots on their records. In the music business, they are called producers. Salsa was undoubtedly the first Latin music style where production values were of paramount importance. Salsa received a tremendous amount of attention because of the promotion it was given by those who had a financial stake in its success. Due in part to successful promotion, salsa spread throughout the Caribbean, to South America, Central America, Europe and the Far East. Local bands sprang up in the most unlikely places, such as Japan and Denmark.

In many ways, salsa became the creation of Fania Records. In the late 1960s Fania began to distribute records under their own label as well as those of smaller independent Latin music recording companies. Fania Records was started by Jerry Masucci, with Johnny Pacheco as musical director. Fania had an interest in controlling the direction of the music it helped spawn and distribute world-wide so successfully. As a result, artists were discouraged from straying from the sounds they were known for. Some, such as critic Larry Birnbaum, feel that attitudes such as these have put a noose on the creativity of the music:

> Like most contemporary genres, salsa has become more of a
> business than a medium for creativity. Even such moderate
> risk-takers as La Sonora Ponceña are closely constrained by
> the culturally conservative international market, and many for-
> ward-looking Latin musicians have turned to jazz as an outlet
> for frustrated artistic ambitions.[15]

Many believe that the promoters of salsa tried to give the false im-
pression that something entirely new had come into being. Naturally,
this effort was in the mainstream of American advertising, which is always coming up with claims of newness and uniqueness. But the result was that it offended many Cubans, both inside and outside of
Cuba. When Fania artists recorded songs by Cuban composers, they
made a policy of not listing the names. In the spaces on the record and
on the album cover where the name of the composer usually goes were
simply the initials D.R., meaning Derechos Reservados—Reserved
Rights. The idea was that, due to the break in relations between the
United States and Cuba, the composers would receive the moneys due
them whenever relations between the two countries improved. As a
result, the general public was not made aware of the tremendous
amount of material by Cuban composers recorded by Fania artists.
For example, on Ray Barretto's 1973 album, the wonderful "Indestructible," half of the eight songs on that album are listed as D.R. In many
instances, knowledgeable people could listen to these recordings and
identify the Cuban source, especially when the songs were by well-
known songwriters such as Ignacio Piñeiro. Consider the following
statement by Santamaria:

> Barretto plays one tune he calls "Guarare." I got a record from
> Cuba which is not sold here. On that record is a tune that is ex-
> actly the same with a Cuban composer.[16]

To add insult to injury, Fania released a movie about the Fania All-
Stars and the salsa scene called "Our Latin Thing (Nuestra Cosa)." It
was the first movie made about Latinos and their music, and starred
the members of the Fania All-Stars and other well-known musicians.
In addition, there is footage of a Santería ceremony and a cockfight
scene.[17] To Cristobal Diaz Ayala, the author of a book written in
Spanish on Cuban popular music, the movie made the suggestion that
salsa had come almost directly from Africa to lodge itself in New York,
thus by-passing Cuba entirely![18]

Instrumentation

The standard salsa instrumentation is a modification of son conjunto. Son conjunto is a musical ensemble which developed before World War II, consisting of two or three trumpets, bongós, a single conga drum, bass, piano and the tres, a Cuban guitar. In addition, a singer might double on guitar. In general, only a single conga drum was played; timbales were not used.

In general, the instrumentation for salsa groups is as follows: one or two lead singers, 2–5 brass instruments, piano, bass, a pair of conga drums, timbales, bongós, a cowbell and various hand-held small percussion instruments. The small percussion are almost invariably assigned to particular members of the ensemble: the bongó player switches to cowbell during part of a piece, and plays an unvarying pattern on the instrument that is an important part of salsa; the lead singer(s) play the other small percussion instruments such as güiro, maracas and claves while they are singing. Frankie Malabe comments on the connection between the small percussion and lead singing:

> It's for your own sake that you learn maracas, güiro, handbell and claves: so you'll become a percussive guy, so you know how to phrase within the rhythm.[21]

The lead singer is accompanied by a coro ("chorus") in the call-and-response pattern which typifies many of the African-derived musics of the New World. There is considerable variation in the instrumentation of the horn section, which tends to have a tougher-sounding quality than that found in earlier styles. Eddie Palmieri started a trend in the early 1960s by using a brass section consisting of two trombones. Both the flute (the European model, rather than the Creole flute used in charanga bands) and the violin have been placed alongside the brass in a few bands. Saxophones are comparatively rare in salsa. Of all the saxophones, the baritone sax seems to be most frequently used, followed by the soprano, tenor and alto in that order.

Perhaps the most unusual band in salsa in terms of instrumentation is Ruben Blades' group, Seis del Solar, with which Oscar Hernández is associated as pianist and arranger. The instrumentation consists of two keyboard players who play synthesizers, piano and/or vibraphone, conga drums, bongós, timbales, trap set and small percussion. Some other types of Latin music ensembles with varying instrumentation will be discussed in PART II: Other Genres Related to Salsa.

Chapter Two

La Clave

In this chapter we will discuss the clave, the rhythmic formula which provides the foundation of salsa. It is only through a thorough appraisal of the relation of clave to every feature that one can see how the parts of the music fit together. The word carries connotations, such as "key," "code," "keystone," which hint at its importance in the music.

The clave is perceived by salsa musicians to be a two measure pattern in $\frac{4}{4}$, or, less frequently, in $\frac{6}{8}$. It is typically performed on the pair of two round sticks known as claves. The late Fernando Ortiz, one of the first to study Afro-Cuban music in depth, claims that the word is derived from "clavija" (wooden peg).[1] The claves are played by a lead singer. Oscar Hernández states that a few timbales players (timbaleros) will occasionally play the pattern on a woodblock. On a recording, the sound produced by the woodblock is sometimes difficult to distinguish from the claves.

The clave is a point of reference for the melody of the singer, the horn (i.e., brass and/or woodwinds) arrangement, the piano figures and the percussion parts. It functions as a point of reference in two ways. On the one hand, the rhythms of the vocal or instrumental parts may simply be identical to the clave with minimal elaboration. In other words, the rests surrounding the clave strokes are filled in by notes. On the other hand, the rhythmic phrase of an individual part may fall on, that is, emphasize, only a few of the five strokes of the clave. Nevertheless, the phrase is accepted as going with the clave. I will provide examples of these phrases in the course of the book.

In salsa, the clave is regarded as beginning as soon as the music begins, and continuing without interruption until the last note. It remains in effect as a centrifugal force throughout the performance of a piece. It continues even when the music is silent during the course of rests, or when breaks in the flow of the arrangement occur. In some bands, a percussionist plays the clave pattern to conduct the start of a piece by giving the time line as a point of reference. John Santos aptly describes all of these attributes as the "clave feeling,"[2] which is nearly universally present in salsa and in the Afro-Cuban musical genres which directly influenced salsa musicians: son, rumba and the religious music of the batá used in Santería. The *clave feeling* is in the music whether or not the *claves* are actually being played.

Hearing the Clave

Although salsa can easily be enjoyed by people who are unable to hear the clave, the experience of listening is definitely enhanced by the ability to hear it. When one taps out the clave pattern along with the music, one gets the sensation of being able to feel the music interact with the clave. In the more rhythmically abstruse music of rumba, continually tapping out the clave is sometimes the only way to keep track of the rhythm. Without tapping the clave, one is thrown off balance by the false perception of other downbeats and meters. The music is enjoyed by knowledgeable listeners in a fashion which recalls a statement of ethnomusicologist John Miller Chernoff about African music:

> It is the listener or dancer who has to supply the beat: the listener must be actively engaged in making sense of the music . . . It is a music-to-find-the-beat-by.[3]

The easiest way to find the clave, of course, is to follow along with the sound of the claves. However, when the texture of the music is complex, it is often surprisingly difficult to trace the relatively quiet, high-pitched sound that the claves produce in the context of a loud band. Often, the sound of the bongós, which is capable of producing a sharp high-pitched sound, resembles the sound of the claves. In rumba, the timbre of the high-tuned quinto drum can also be mistaken for the claves. When the claves are absent, the clave feeling is perceptible in the phrasing of the melody and in other percussion patterns. We will discuss these in greater detail further in the chapter.

The ability to hear the clave is an integral part of a musician's education. Sheller told me that Malabe played an important part in his learning about the music. Coincidentally, Malabe credits Sheller with introducing him to jazz. Sheller began playing in Latin bands, as they were then called, at the beginning of his career, when he was a bur-geoning jazz trumpet player. After being picked by a few Latin bandleaders at the Musicians Union Hall in New York City as a re-placement for the bands' regular trumpet players, Sheller developed a reputation as a non-Hispanic who was very interested in the music. At the time, Latin music was like a foreign language to him. Formerly, his idea of Latin music consisted of the Americanized versions of tunes played at weddings and barmitzvas. He met Malabe in the late 1950s, when they were working together in Arvito's band. Arvito was the stage name for Harvey Averne, who later became active as a salsa record producer.

Sheller and Malabe often got together to play jazz and Latin records. After awhile, Malabe learned that Sheller took a special delight in being able to figure out where the clave was in rhythmically confusing performances. Malabe brought out of his record collection the selec-tions in which it was difficult to hear the "one." At first, Sheller would be completely confused by the rhythm. Malabe would then show him where the beat started and tell him to follow along with the clave. Eventually, Sheller told me, he was able to hear the clave in any music from the oldest son montunos to the most modern Tito Puente arrange-ment. At this point, Malabe played him some batá music and, at first, Sheller felt like he "was back to Square One."

The Son Clave

At this point in the text, I will present only the $^4_4$ form of the clave known as "son clave," but it should be kept in mind that there are other forms as well:

EX. 2.1. *The son clave.*

It can be seen from the above example that the clave is made up of five strokes. Musicians use the terms "going with the clave," "fitting with the clave," "falling on the strokes of the clave" or "lining up with the clave" to discuss the resemblance of a rhythmic phrase with this pattern. It is worthwhile to note that, according to John Amira and Frankie Malabe, although the five strokes do not have individual names, anything that accentuates the second stroke of the clave is called the 'bombo.' The name is that of the bass drum played in comparsa, the Afro-Cuban Carnival music, which emphasizes that stroke.

Like other two-measure percussion patterns used in salsa, the clave pattern can be presented in a way that musicians call "beginning with either measure," or "reversed." Note that in the example below, the second measure of the clave is followed by the first measure:

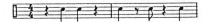

EX. 2.2. *Son clave, reverse form.*

Arranging a Melody in Clave

In salsa, a melody can begin on the first or second measure of the clave, depending upon how it fits best with the five strokes of the clave. Melodies which begin with the first measure, the one with the three strokes, are described by salsa musicians as being in 3–2 clave; those that begin with the second measure, with the two strokes, as being in 2–3 clave. Marty Sheller, Oscar Hernández and other arrangers make a practice of indicating "2–3 clave" or "3–2 clave" at the top of their scores. The 2–3 clave is also, but less frequently, called reverse clave. Each of the two measures is distinguished from the other by such words as "side," "part" or "section." For example, a musician will speak of the "2 part" of the clave.

In order to avoid confusion, when I use the word 'clave' without using the terminology 3–2 or 2–3, it should be understood as the 3–2 form. By extension, when I refer to a particular stroke of the clave— say, for example, the fourth stroke—I am counting from the first stroke in the 3 part of the clave.

In order to write a salsa arrangement, the arranger must know what form the clave is in—whether the song is in 2–3 or 3–2 clave. Whenever possible, Sheller tells the songwriter to submit a recording of the song with someone tapping the clave in the background. According to Sheller, the songs that musicians used to perform had a much more clearly defined clave feeling. Now, some songs sound as if they could be arranged with either form of the clave, due to the influence of music other than salsa on the songwriters. In addition, some artists want the arranger to convert an already composed song from another tradition in salsa style. Sheller told me that he has developed a reputation for arranging this type of material. For example, Sheller did an arrangement of "Dancing Cheek to Cheek" which resulted in a popular hit for the artists, a salsa band with the unlikely name of The Bad Street Boys. Sheller has two ways of approaching material of this nature. First of all, he sings the melody and taps out both forms of the cáscara pattern (see Example 2.10 a & b). Although the song may fit without too many obvious problems in either way, Sheller finds that one way usually sounds better than the other. Sheller also tries to find a phrase in the melody that closely fits the clave.

> Usually somewhere in the course of the song there is a phrase
> that makes the form of the clave obvious. Then you work back
> from there to see how the other phrases fit. And if there's a
> phrase that goes against the clave, then you have to make some
> kind of alteration such as adding or subtracting one bar here or
> there. It can usually be done in a subtle way so that it sounds
> hip. I'll try to put something in there that makes the melody fit
> into the clave in a musical way so that people who are dancing
> are not going to realize that it "turned around" there—even
> though a musician will realize it. It just flows along.

Arrangers are recognized and respected for their ability to write music that flows well with the clave. Malabe told me of one well-known arranger in the Latin jazz field who would customarily bring his arrangements to René Hernández to check whether or not the music was in clave. (René Hernández developed his name as one of Machito's best known arrangers; he later arranged for Eddie Palmieri.) For Oscar Hernández (no relation to René), the skill of arranging in clave is different than the ability to play the piano in clave. As a pianist, he tends to make up phrases based on whether they intuitively feel right in a particular context. When he started to do arranging, however, he had to develop the ability to see on paper the figures that work best with the clave:

> In my earlier recordings I wasn't really aware of the clave. I was just playing naturally: playing a certain way rhythmically because it felt right. There are guys out there who have a perfect feeling for the clave and don't understand what they're doing. When I really started arranging I became aware why some things work and certain rhythmic figures don't work. The first things I wrote, there were things that were out of clave. Seeing it on paper focused me on the importance of the clave.

Oddly-Phrased Melodies

It would be easier to keep track of the clave if all salsa arrangements were based entirely on two-measure melodic phrases, or on phrases whose lengths are multiples of two. Many are, but some are not. A single measure, or a phrase with an odd number of measures, or a one-measure rest will give the melody a new relation to the clave. Sheller is particularly good at adding an extra measure at the end of one section, so that the next section begins on the other measure of the clave. Sheller explains it in these words:

> Once the song begins and the clave starts, the clave never changes. But the 'one' may change. Clave is a 2 measure phrase. So it may change from the feeling of the '1' being on the first beat of the 2 part of the clave to the first beat of the 3 part of the clave.

There are also songs in which the tonic and dominant chords fall on the fourth beat for several measures in a row, tricking the listener into thinking that the fourth beat is really the first beat. The listener may then incorrectly tap the clave a beat too early. The noted tres player and band leader Arsenio Rodriguez was famous for composing songs with this quality. In the refrain to "Dolorcito de mi China," recorded by Rodriguez in the 1940s and re-recorded by Larry Harlow in the 1970s, the harmonies change on the fourth beats on both of the measures of the repeated phrase seen in Ex. 2.3.

EX. 2.3. *Excerpt of an Arsenio Rodriguez melody.*

The following example is transcribed from a recent recording by Los Van Van, an influential and popular Cuban group. Here, the harmonies change on the fourth beat of the first and third measures—to the tonic and dominant chords respectively. Because of the placement of the chords, the melody sounds as if it were not in $\frac{4}{4}$, but in a repeated pattern of $\frac{3}{4}$, $\frac{5}{4}$, $\frac{3}{4}$, $\frac{5}{4}$, etc.

EX. 2.4. *Excerpt from a Los Van Van melody.*

When I first heard this selection, I was unable to determine on which beat it began. It was not until I tried to transcribe it that I was able to figure it out. I began with the assumption that it was in $\frac{4}{4}$, since the vast majority of salsa arrangements are in that meter. I also knew that the rhythm was based on clave, so I looked for rhythmic phrases that are common in either part of the clave. Eventually I arrived at the correct transcription and evaluation of how the melody fit with the clave. At that time, I brought the recording and my transcription to Sheller's attention. To my amazement, he immediately tapped out the clave. It seemed that, where I was fooled by the harmonic downbeats, he could quickly pinpoint the rhythmic phrase behind the accents created by harmonic changes.

La Clave: Part I

In order to illustrate some aspects of clave, we have transcribed the verse of a song composed by Joe Torres entitled *La Clave*, from a 1976 recording by the well-known Puerto Rican-based group, La Sonora Ponceña. This group, whose name means "the sound of Ponce," a city in Puerto Rico, has been in existence for many years. It features the talents of pianist and arranger Papo Lucca, who, along with pianist Eddie Palmieri, succeeded in bringing a sophisticated jazz-influenced harmonic vocabulary to salsa in the 1960s.

The song is in a relaxed, slow-to-medium tempo known as son montuno, a tempo generally slower than the majority of salsa pieces, which tend to be fast. I have transcribed only the lead singer's part. Luigui Texidor was the singer. Several phrases in the song were sung in a choral style. For example, the phrase with the vocables "A la, a la, a la" (measures four through eight), was sung with the chorus, which included Hector LaVoe, Ruben Blades, Tito Allen and Ray de la Paz—all well-known recording artists themselves. This particular passage is reminiscent of Arsenio Rodriguez, the most popular exponent of son montunos; I have heard the same phrase, with the same melody and harmonization, on a recording of an Arsenio Rodriguez composition by Justi Barretto.

> *The boys asked me to sing a son montuno. A la, a la, a la. For the people who know how to appreciate from the heart, to admire with emotion, trying to understand, knowing that way out in the country is where the key exists, where they set down the clave from the moon to the sun [i.e., night to day]. I felt great admiration and I began to compose [two times], to let the people know, without luxury or details, but with feeling, honouring the moment that was granted me, without being polite to the two-faced people who say they come hungry to taste the salad, and after they have been provided for, say nothing was happening.*

La Clave

Joe Torres

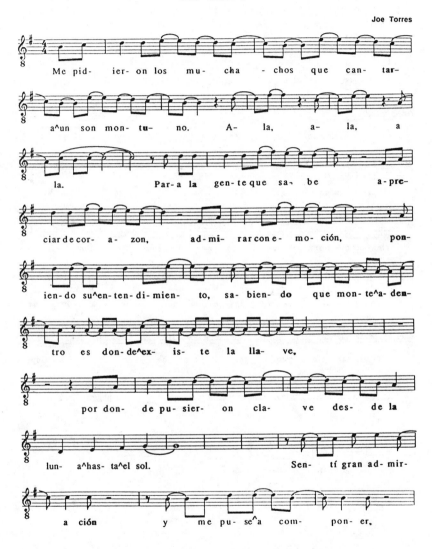

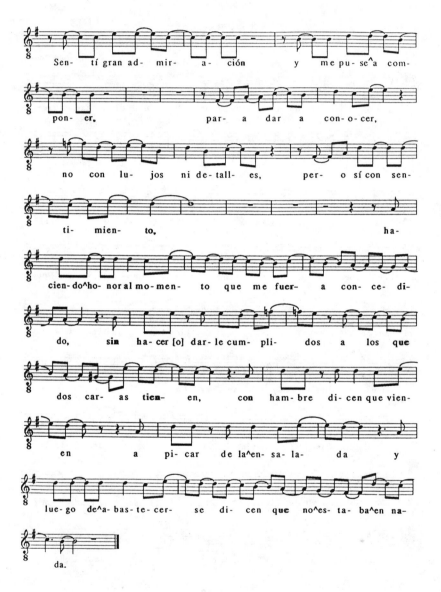

Sen- tí gran ad- mir- a- ción y me pu- se^a com-

pon- er, par- a dar a con- o- cer,

no con lu- jos ni de- tall- es, per- o sí con sen-

ti- mien- to, ha-

cien- do^ho- nor al mo- men- to que me fuer- a con- ce- di-

do, sin ha- cer [o] dar- le cum- pli- dos a los que

dos car- as tien- en, con ham- bre di- cen que vien-

en a pi- car de la^en- sa- la- da y

lue- go de^a- bas- te- cer- se di- cen que no^es- ta- ba^en na-

da.

The song is in 2–3 clave. There is only one two-measure segment in the entire song that coincides with four of the five strokes of the clave:

Ex. 2.5. *Excerpt A from "La Clave."*

The first measure in the excerpt above (measures 26–27 in the full transcription) is the three part of the clave followed by the two part. Note that the first note is tied over from the previous measure; the first stroke of the clave is anticipated. In fact, the majority of the measures in the song which fall on the three part of the clave (the second, fourth, sixth, eighth, tenth measures, etc.) begin with a note that is tied over from the previous measure. Rhythms in which beat one is anticipated are very common in salsa melodies and piano figures.

The song is filled with a rhythmic pattern that begins in the two part of the clave as follows:

EX. 2.6. *Common rhythmic pattern in "La Clave."*

The harmony changes on the last note of the pattern. Here is an example from the ninth measure of the song transcription:

Ex. 2.7. *Excerpt B from "La Clave."*

Melodies and piano figures based on this rhythmic pattern are very common in salsa. They often begin on the two part of the clave. The measure which follows this rhythmic pattern typically is filled with notes falling on the off-beats. One of the most standard piano and tres figures in salsa, made famous by tres player Arsenio Rodriguez, begins with the same pattern, and continues with four more notes, all falling on off-beats:

2 Part   3 Part

EX. 2.8. *Arsenio Rodriguez figure.*

The pattern coincides with only two strokes of the clave. The reason that the pattern fits with 2–3 clave can be interpreted two ways: 1) that it has become accepted in this manner; and/or 2) because, other than the first beat, the first measure has the only note—it happens to be the second note of the phrase—which falls right on the beat, and that beat happens to be on the second beat, one of the clave strokes.

A few other phrases in the song transcription likewise begin on the two part of the clave. In these phrases, a note coincides with the clave stroke on the third beat of the first measure:

ien-do su^en-ten-di-mien-

EX. 2.9. *Excerpt C from "La Clave."*

Clave "Substitutes"

There are other unvarying two-measure patterns besides the clave. When the claves are not played, it is these patterns that tell the musicians where the clave is. Like the clave, these patterns are reversible, so that they can begin on either measure. At this point we will briefly describe two unvarying, two-measure patterns which can act as substitutes for the claves in the role of providing the clave. The first pattern is called cáscara; the second is the pattern typically played by the hand-held cowbell.

The cáscara (lit. "rind, shell") is a rhythm played with two sticks ("palitos") on the side of the conga or on a woodblock in rumba, or on the sides of the timbales drums in a salsa group. This is the cáscara rhythm:

EX. 2.10a. *Cáscara in 2–3 clave.*

EX. 2.10b. *Cáscara in 3–2 clave.*

In Havana, the rhythm is also called cáscara, but in some areas of Cuba it has other names: in Matanzas, gua-gua (lit. "trivial thing") and in Santiago de Cuba, catá.[4] Note that points of the cáscara pattern coincide with the first, second, fourth and fifth strokes of the son clave:

EX. 2.11. *Points of convergence between the cáscara and the son clave.*

The hand-held cowbell is played by the bongó player. In salsa arrangements, the bongó player puts down the bongós and begins playing the cowbell in the section variously known as the montuno or coro ("chorus") section. Using a hammer shaft as a beater, the bongó player produces a strong, low sound and a high, weak sound to create the typical cowbell pattern. Strokes played over the rim of the bell make the low sound; those on the closed end of the bell, the high sound. In the example below, the high sound is written on the top space of the staff:

Ex. 2.12a. *Bell pattern in 2–3 clave.*

Ex. 2.12b. *Bell pattern in 3–2 clave.*

Note that points of the bell pattern coincide with all five strokes of the clave:

EX. 2.13. *Points of congruence between the bell pattern and the son clave.*

The Absence of Clave

At any measure of a salsa piece, except in the slow bolero, there is almost always a clave feeling. But this does not mean that every percussion instrument, every vocal line, every bass line, every piano figure and every horn part at that particular measure could be isolated and still show a relation to the clave. Some phrases are not "split up," as Malabe puts it. In other words, the pattern is only one measure long, and the same thing is played in the 2 part of the clave as the 3 part. For example, the cowbell pattern transcribed in Example 2.12b is often performed in Cuba, according to Malabe, with the bongó player repeating just the first measure of the 3–2 pattern.

In addition, the clave feeling in Latin jazz, the cousin of salsa which was developed by Machito and his associate, Mario Bauza, along with the team of Dizzy Gillespie and conga legend, Chano Pozo, is occasionally absent in bebop phrases when the jazz spirit is sometimes considered more important than the clave feeling. For example, a Latin jazz tune by Sheller recently recorded by Lew Soloff contains phrases that, from a salsa perspective, sound out of clave. As the composer, he considered the jazz quality of this particular piece to be more important than the clave.

The Clave Sensibility

Musicians seem to have primarily two different ways they understand the importance of clave feeling when they evaluate a performance: as a sort of grammar with fixed rules, and as a flexible rhythmic sensibility. On the one hand, musicians speak about a performance being "right" or "wrong," or "cruzao." On the other hand, they say that something may not feel right to them, but that doesn't mean that it should be condemned. At times, mistakes in the execution of the clave are put out on a recording before the musician realizes that he or she has made a mistake, and tries to correct it. Although technically incorrect in terms of clave, Malabe feels that it probably wouldn't sound bad in the context of a full group:

> When you're playing in a band and sometimes the tune might
> sound both ways—that's where it gets a little tricky. As a result
> sometimes the drummer might make a mistake. It's a natural
> thing—I've done it. Sometimes the tune sounds like it's 'this
> way.' And then after you hear the tune, you'll say: 'Oh no,

> it's the other way around.' And sometimes it's too late. But it's
> not a question of that it's going to sound bad. No, it's not a
> question of that. It's a question of that *you* made the mistake,
> and drummers who do the folklore *know* it. And that's a small
> crowd.

When musicians believe that a phrase does not work well rhythmically with the clave, they say it is "out of clave," or "off–clave." When
a phrase sounds like it is played on the wrong measure of the clave—
say, on the 3 part of the clave instead of the 2 part—the clave is said to
be "cruzao" (shortened form of "cruzado") meaning "crossed."
Musicians are not always in agreement about whether or not a phrase
is "in clave."

Amira comments on a kind of nagging disturbance in his response
to the music that leads him to think that the music is off-clave:

> I'll be listening to a piece of music, not specifically focusing
> on any one thing. But something will be irritating me, almost
> like when you have something inside your clothing that's stick-
> ing you and you're absent-mindedly trying to get it off your
> skin. Eventually it protrudes so strongly that I find myself as-
> king "What's wrong with this?" And, of course, the first
> thing I'll check is the clave.

The following two examples provide an exercise in hearing the proper
placement of the clave rhythm. In considering them, Sheller and Hernández agreed that the boxed-in areas of the following selections were
off-clave.

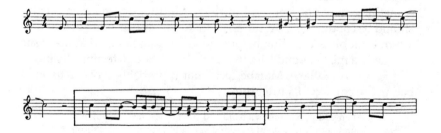

Ex. 2.14. *Off-clave exercise A.*

The above selection was sung with several other voices singing in harmony (not shown). The boxed-in measures are performed without the steady eighth-note background that comes as a result of the composite patterns of the congas, bongós, timbales and maracas. Sheller noted that with the accompaniment, these measures would not sound so "crossed." As it is, there is an emphasis on the "and" after the second beat of the two part of the clave, but no emphasis on that point in the three part, where the bombo is supposed to fall. In terms of the clave, the measures sound almost as if they should have been switched around.

Ex. 2.15. *Off-clave exercise B̲.*

The selection in Ex. 2.15 was performed by a brass instrument, with an additional horn playing a harmony part below not shown. The boxed-in measures are performed as a *cierre* ("break"), with all the instruments playing in rhythmic unison along with the horns. In terms of the clave, the two measures sound, as in Ex. 2.14, as if they should have been switched around. Again, there is an emphasis on the "and" after the second beat of the two part of the clave, but no emphasis on that point in the three part, where the bombo is supposed to fall.

In concluding the discussion of the clave, we can do no better than to quote Tito Puente:

> You have to fit into a clave beat—those two little sticks.
> Everybody has to play with the clave; if one musician is not
> playing in clave, it disturbs your hearing.[5]

La Inspiración

The inspiración, or improvised lyric, a characteristic trait of much Afro-Caribbean music, is the meat and potatoes of the salsa singer's performance. Here, he or she quotes from the coro phrase, or comments on the topic of the song or the events taking place in the performance arena. The inspiration (the English translation is widely accepted) may not necessarily follow a logical development of one topic or idea, and may contain extraneous material. While the verse is typically in standard Spanish, the inspirations are laden with slang and street language.

In a salsa arrangement, the lead singer improvises his or her text in the montuno section, which follows directly after the verse. In this section, also called the coro section, the piano plays a repeated pattern, usually four or eight measures long, known as a guajeo or montuno, over which the textual/melodic improvisations take place in alternation with an unvarying choral phrase. The choral phrase, known as the coro, and each statement of the lead singer are the same length as the guajeo. The lead singer thus has only a few bars to make up an effective textual and melodic statement in a rhythmically compelling fashion.

Salsa singers typically emphasize the off-beats when they are singing their inspirations. Amira notes that in the folkloric singing style, especially as represented by the Conjunto Guaguancó Matancero, the feeling is much more haphazard-sounding and rhythmically unpredictable.

La Clave: Part II

In order to give an example of the inspiration, I have transcribed the remainder of the text of *La Clave*, beginning directly after the verse with the beginning of the coro section. The coro part goes as follows: "Don't skip the clave there, that's where the key is."

Ex. 2.16. *Coro of "La Clave."*

Each statement of the lead singer, indicated by a dash in the transcription below, follows the coro each time. The Spanish transcription is followed by a loose translation, done with the aid of Frankie Malabe; the meaning of the text is not always readily apparent. Note the use of the word "guapo," a word which in Spain and some parts of Latin America simply means "handsome, pretty, lovely," etc., depending upon the sex of the person described and the person doing the describing. Among Puerto Ricans and other people, however, the word has several other meanings: it could be used to describe a "tough guy" or a "slick dude."

The Inspirational Statements

—Oye, caballero, si tu no sabes me hablas, es mejor que tu te calles.
—Aqui no se brinca tabla. Aqui nadie brinca; todo el mundo lleva la clave.
—Brinca la tablita que yo la brinque. Avanza y brincala ahora o te viro la patas al reves.
—Es donde existe la clave. Ahí el que entra nunca sale.
—Caballero, en ese barrio donde yo vivo, ahí los guapos, los guapos no caben.
—Aunque dios no me dio belleza, me dio bastante sabor. Me pintó de este color y me dio tremenda cabeza para meterle la clave.
—En mi barrio todo el mundo es tranquilo. No vaya guapeando porque de ahí tu no sales.
—No vaya con miel de abaja.
—Todo el mundo habla del negro, pero nadie me dice de donde el negro sale.
—Avanza y brincala tu ahora o te viro las patas en reves.
—Yo soy negro tranquilo. Es mejor que no me chaves.

—*Listen, gentlemen, if you don't know what you're talking about, it is better that you be quiet.*
—*Don't skip the board here. Here no one is skipping; everyone has the clave.*
—*Jump the little board where I jumped. Go ahead and jump now or I'll twist your knees around.*
—*That is where the clave exists. Whoever enters never comes out.*
—*Mister, in that neighborhood where I live, there the slick dudes, the slick dudes don't belong.*

—Although God did not give me beauty, he gave me plenty of zest. He painted me this color and gave me an understanding of the clave.
—In my neighborhood everyone is calm. Don't go being a slick dude because from there you don't come out.
—Don't go being falsely sweet.
—Everybody talks about the Black, but nobody tells me where Blackness comes from.
—Go ahead and jump it now or I'll twist your knees around.
—I'm a tranquil guy. It is better that you don't mess with me.

As a reading of the lyrics of *La Clave* demonstrate, the song texts communicate many matters concerning the environment from which they are derived. Supported by the music, the nature of Hispanic street culture in the Caribbean and the United States is strongly and unashamedly put forth.

Chapter Three

Los Instrumentos: Part I

Salsa is based on the rhythms of the percussion instruments. In addition, the bass and piano supply a rhythmic force which interacts with the other percussion instruments. In effect, the bass and piano in salsa have an important rhythmic function as well as a harmonic one. In the next two chapters, I will introduce the members of the salsa rhythm section, beginning with the piano and bass.

The Piano

Latin piano playing has three different components: the rhythmic accompaniment known as guajeo, written passages played in unison with the bass, and the improvised piano solo. In the same way that Nuyoricans alternate between Spanish and English when they are speaking to another Nuyorican, the modern salsa pianist alternates between the típica style and a jazz style in which the right hand takes the lead while the left hand supplies jazz-style chordal figures.

The most influential architects of the típica style, according to Hernández, are Lily Martínez Griñan, pianist with Arsenio Rodriguez, and Jésus Perez, pianist with the famous flutist and charanga bandleader Arcaño. Both gained recognition in the 1940s. Hernández mentions pianist Peruchin as another important influence on Latin pianists of the 1950s and 1960s. Peruchin was a pianist with a generally light touch who demonstrated a firm grasp of jazz harmony. In an almost schizophrenic manner, he would begin a jazz standard such as "All the Things You Are" and give it an Errol Garner-style interpretation, although with a definitely original sound. After the tune was played, in-

Photograph courtesy of Oscar Hernández.

Pianist Oscar Hernández with the Pete "El Conde" Rodriguez group.

stead of continuing in the jazz mode of improvising on the harmonic framework of the tune, Peruchin might jump right into a decidedly Latin groove that had nothing to do with the original tune.

The Guajeo

The guajeo is a repeated phrase, usually two, four or eight measures long. The phrase typically covers a short range, usually less than an octave, and emphasizes the off-beats. It is also called montuno, and is played as an accompaniment to the coro or to solos by a horn player or percussionist. According to Sheller, English-speaking musicians at times may simply call it the vamp. During the montuno section, the pianist always plays a guajeo, but the arranger might also call for a guajeo at certain points of the guía, or verse section. In some recordings, the pianist plays a note-for-note repetition of the phrase, while in others, the pianist makes slight changes while consistently maintaining the general melodic ideas. Hernández believes that an approach of making few or no changes is the correct way of performing a guajeo:

> The piano plays an important part of the rhythm section. You
> have to play rhythmically something that will make it swing.
> You can't be changing every 2 or 3 bars. You can change from
> section to section, and sometimes it's advisable to change from
> section to section to bring the music to another level. That's the
> correct way of doing it, that you're only going to change from
> section to section to heighten the excitement of the music. But
> you don't change other than that. To me, that separates some-
> one professional from someone immature. I don't do anything
> more than what's asked for—to rhythmically lay down what
> I'm supposed to. You have to perform as a unit—a team player.

Hernández' statement reveals the importance he ascribes to pattern
consistency, an esthetic judgement expressed to me by Frankie Malabe
in speaking of the right way to come out of the rhythmic unison figures
in a cierre ("break"). The point is that Latin music reaches its richest
moments, its "swing," because of the ways that several ostinatos (or
partial ostinatos) played simultaneously, each with its own rhythmic
values, grind against or support each other. Hernández believes the
pianist should stick closely to his/her own ostinato phrase, rather than
creating a constantly changing accompaniment in the fashion of a jazz
pianist in a bebop group. The Latin pianist figures out a guajeo that
fits underneath the melody given to the coro in a particular arrangement, and sticks to it for subsequent performances of the arrangement.
For the most part, guajeos are not written out. But Sheller often writes
out a guajeo figure for sight-reading purposes which fits with the coro.
Nevertheless, he is perfectly happy for the pianist to go beyond this
guide and create his/her own guajeo. The word montuneando is
sometimes used to describe the process of playing guajeos.

Stylistic Characteristics

In the típica style the guajeos are played in octaves, or in tenths with
an occasional eleventh. Hernández states that some pianists play with
a big sound using tripled or quadrupled octaves and filled-in diatonic
chords. In certain contexts, Hernández plays a guajeo in a jazz style by
using a jazz harmonic palette of sound, instead of the diatonic approach of the típica style:

Ex. 3.1. *Jazz-style guajeo.*

The Guajeo: 2–3 Clave Versions

The direction of the clave influences the rhythmic shape of the guajeo. After repeated hearing, it becomes clear that guajeos played for 2–3 clave sound different than those for 3–2 clave, but the differences are subtle. In 2–3 clave, it is very common for the guajeo to begin with the following rhythmic outline:

Ex. 3.2. *Rhythmic outline of 2–3 clave, first measure.*

The rhythmic nature of the guajeo is influenced by where the harmonic downbeats fall: on the first and last notes of the above example—on beats one, and on the "and" after beat four, respectively. The subsequent measure begins on the "and" after beat one. When played in a legato style, the fourth note is held over to the subsequent measure.

Ex. 3.3. *Guajeo phrase A in 2–3 clave.*

The guajeo played in Ex. 3.3 is in 2–3 clave, and is typically repeated with few or no alterations for the duration of a section in a salsa arrangement. Note that, although both measures contain off-beat phrasing, the second measure of each example, the three part of the clave, is somewhat more syncopated than the first. As Amira once explained to me, the two measures of the clave stand together as a balance, and the relation between more syncopated and less syncopated is evident in the example. Another reason that the phrase works in 2–3 clave is that beat two is emphasized in the two part of the clave, while the "and" after beat two, known as the "bombo," is emphasized in the three part.

One common rhythmic pattern which occurs in guajeos in 2–3 clave, as well in melodies in 2–3 clave such as Tito Puente's "Saca Tu Mujer," is exhibited in the following example:

Ex. 3.4. *Guajeo phrase B in 2–3 clave.*

Guajeos: 3–2 Clave Versions

In an interview, I asked Hernández to play a phrase that would fit in 3–2 clave. He asked me to clap the clave to give him the right impetus, and he played a guajeo with his right hand. At the same time, in his left hand he played the part which a bass player would employ to accompany it. The fact that Hernández was listening to a time line (the clave) at the same time he came up with two entirely different rhythmic patterns—one for a pianist, the other for a bassist—brought to mind the sort of rhythmic acuity possessed by the West African musicians from whom John Miller Chernoff learned:

> Only through the combined rhythms does the music emerge,
> and the only way to hear the music properly . . . is to listen to at
> least two rhythms at once.[1]

Although it is not difficult for a pianist fluent in reading music to play the phrase with the bass part, it was the ability to execute it without preparation that impressed me. I believe that this ability is shared by many professional musicians in the Latin music world. For example, Amira states that when there are not enough drummers in a folkloric group, at least one of the drummers can replicate the sounds of drum parts that are typically handled by another drummer, in addition to his or her own part.

Here is the guajeo as realized by Hernández, arranged for piano (top two staves) and bass (bottom stave):

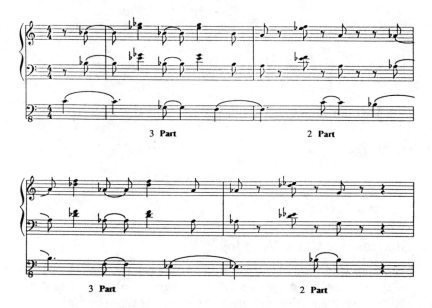

Ex. 3.5. *Guajeo phrase C in 3–2 clave.*

In the above example, the notes in the three part of the clave fall on the off-beats, while in the two part, the first three notes fall on beats one, two and three. The harmonic downbeats occur only in the two part of the clave, on beat one and on the "and" after four. I have heard guajeos following the rhythmic outline of the above example on numerous recordings by several different pianists. Often, the two part of the clave is filled in with more eighth notes, but the rhythmic thrust is similar.

After the initial measure of the 3–2 guajeo figure in the following example, the off-beats are stressed in both measures of the clave, and harmonic downbeats occur on the "and" after the fourth beats of every measure:

Ex.3.6a. *Guajeo phrase D in 3–2 clave.*

As soon as Hernández finished playing this phrase, I decided to play the Devil's Advocate, and ask him why the above example couldn't be played in 2–3 clave just as well as in 3–2. After telling me to clap the clave again, he gave me a musical answer:

Ex. 3.6b. *Variation of guajeo phrase $\underline{D}$ in 2–3 clave.*

What Hernández had done was to transpose the theme of the melody of the 3–2 guajeo, and put it into 2–3! Note the presence of the following rhythmic outline, notated and discussed above, in the two part of the clave:

Ex. 3.7. *Rhythmic outline of 2 part of the clave.*

Other Guajeos

I asked Hernández whether there were some guajeos that could be played for both the 2–3 and 3–2 forms of the clave. I played a recording in which Hernández played the following guajeo:

Ex. 3.8. *Guajeo for both forms of the clave.*

Hernández agreed that the above guajeo could be played in either form of the clave, and that there were "definitely" other guajeos of a similar nature.

Piano Solos

After the call-and-response interchanges between the lead singer, or a horn player, and the coro in the montuno section, the pianist is sometimes given an extended solo. He or she is accompanied only by the other members of the rhythm section—the conga drums, bongós, timbales and the bass. Hernández enumerates the characteristics of salsa piano solos:

> Stylistically, you have the octaves and the staggering of the octaves, which is a Latin trademark. That's a whole art in itself. You have both hands doing the same thing a lot in Latin piano playing. It's diatonic. Latin pianists do repeated riffs that interplay with the rhythm section.

The Bass

The bass has a more percussive role in salsa than in jazz. Andy González, who is perhaps the most well-known acoustic bass player in salsa, states:

> In Latin music you have to approach the bass as a drummer
> would approach the drums—with the same sense of percussive-
> ness and attacks . . . A bass player is a drummer. Even in jazz
> they're still hung up on the harmonic aspects and don't see the
> rhythmic potential.[2]

The Cuban-born bassist Cachao (born in 1916 with the name Israel
Lopez) helped develop this approach, along with his other contribu-
tions to Latin music as a composer and bandleader. As in a jazz group,
the Latin bassist and pianist is given a lead sheet with written figures
in some spots and chord symbols in the others. The performer execut-
ing the part is expected to fill in the measures where there are only
chord symbols with an improvised part. Nine times out of ten, the
Latin bassist will almost automatically interpret a series of chord symbols—popularly known as "chord changes"—by the harmonic device
of anticipation. Consider the following example:

Ex. 3.9. *Anticipation in a bass line.*

The harmonies change on the fourth beat of every measure. On the
fourth beat of the first measure, for example, the bass moves to D, the
fifth of the G chord. In many performances, the bassist changes harmonies before the pianist. For while he or she makes the change on the
fourth beat, the pianist often changes to the next chord either a half
beat later (on the "and" after four) or a full beat later (on the first beat).
This divergence in harmonic change has the effect of emphasizing, or
accenting, different spots in the music, thus subtly adding to the basic
polyrhythmic quality of this music.

The bass player does not always play anticipating bass lines. Following are two examples of non-anticipatory bass lines:

Ex. 3.10. *Other bass lines.*

The bassist usually emphasizes one or both of two rhythmic points: the fourth beat and the "and" after the second beat. He or she is often accenting the same places as the conga player.

Rhythmically speaking, these examples of bass lines are all one measure long. As a result, the same rhythm is played in the two part as in the three part of the clave. When a two measure pattern is played with different rhythmic values in each measure, the bassist—or the arranger when there is a written part for the bass—shapes the line so that it fits the clave. Consider the following example, which is a written bass line played in unison with the piano during the mambo section of a piece recorded by La Sonora Ponceña:

Ex. 3.11. *Two measure bass line.*

In conclusion, the bass has several functions: to act as the harmonic anchor for the group, to reinforce the tumbao, the standard conga drum figure, and to create its own rhythmic part. From a rhythmic perspective, bass lines are one or two measure ostinatos. When they are two measures long, they are rooted in the clave.

Chapter Four

Los Instrumentos: Part II

The Conga Drum

The conga drum is a single-headed drum with a tapered barrel shape. The shell is traditionally made of wood; in the last few decades, some models have been made of fiberglass. The advantage of the fiberglass is a louder sound, but these drums often lack the rich sound of the wooden models. The skin is made of calf, mule or cow's skin; it is held in place by tuning lugs.[1] The conga drum comes in three sizes. The distance from the base of the drum to the skin remains the same; the variables are the fatness of the drum and the width of the head. Salsa musicians refer to the collective family of these drums as conga drums, congas, tumbas or tumbadoras.

The smallest drum is called quinto. The name is derived from re-quinto, a name also given to the similarly high-pitched drum used in the Puerto Rican bomba and plena. The choice of this word for the highest pitched drum in the conga drum family seems to come from the high clarinets used in military bands, whose Spanish name is re-quinto.[2] The middle drum is given various names, including conga, segunda and tres golpes. The largest drum is called the tumbadora. The average width of the drum heads is as follows: the quinto, 11 inches; the segunda, 11 3/4 inches; and the tumbadora, 12 1/2 inches.[3] The tuning of the drums is not standardized, and varies according to the player and the musical situation. The Spanish name for someone who plays conga drums is "conguero."

The conga drum is a Cuban instrument said to be derived from the Bantu or Congolese drum ensemble called ngoma,[4] which is still played in Cuba. Besides its use in a wide range of popular musics throughout the world, it is used in the Congolese-derived religious groups in Cuba called Palo, or more specifically, Palo Monte, Palo Briyumba, Palo Mayomba and Palo Kimbisa.[5] Arsenio Rodriguez was a Palero, and held Palo ceremonies with his brothers, according to Amira. It is also used in Santería, the Yoruba-derived religion from Cuba which has many adherents there and in Puerto Rico, New York, and Miami. Its acceptance in popular Cuban music is more recent than one might imagine. It was not really until the late 1930s and early 1940s that the conga drum was successfully integrated into the Latin rhythm section, an innovation credited to Arsenio Rodriguez. The late singer Machito (1908–1984, né Francisco [also Frank] Grillo) is regarded as the leader of the first band in New York to introduce the conga drum as a regular member of the rhythm section.[6]

Before this time, the two ensembles which exerted the greatest influence on the evolution of salsa—the charanga and the various son groups known as sextetos and septetos—did not use conga drums. The son groups featured the bongós along with hand-held percussion instruments such as the claves, the güiro and the maracas. The charanga used the timbales and the güiro. The drums were used primarily in the aforementioned Afro-Cuban religions and in the secular genre known as rumba, which is played by an ensemble consisting of the three members of the conga drum family—the quinto, the segunda and the tumbadora—in addition to a few small percussion instruments and singers.

Playing Position

In traditional Afro-Cuban music, conga drums are played one per each player. There is usually more than one player in the group, each playing a differently sized instrument. However, in popular music (referred to as "band music" by Amira and Malabe) there is rarely more than one conguero in the ensemble. During the first decade of the conga drum's membership in the rhythm section of popular bands, only one conga drum was played by the conguero. From the 1950s on, congueros have played two conga drums, and there are some who play three or more. When only one drum is played, it is held between the knees and tipped a bit forward so the sound can come out of the bottom of the drum. When two drums are played, the higher-pitched of the two is held between the knees while the lower one rests alongside it to the right. The majority of strokes on the lower drum are played by the right hand. Some musicians give the two drums the names macho (male), for the smaller of the pair, and hembra (female), for the larger. Conga drums are sometimes mounted on stands which raise them off the ground. In this case, the conguero plays them in a standing position.

Hand Positions

There are primarily two types of sounds: open tones and closed tones, which are played in a variety of hand positions. Amira enumerates the following closed tones: the muff, the slap, the palm and the touch. On band recordings, the open tones are often the only audible sounds. In the open tone, the last joint hits the head of the drum as all the fingers of the hand except the thumb hit the drum in a flat position. The fingers are held together so there is no space between them. Immediately after striking, the fingers rebound, with the palm still resting on the edge of the drum. With the muff, the position for the open tones is used; the difference is that the fingers do not rebound, thus creating a muted effect. The bass is created by striking the center of the drum with the hand in a cupped position. The lower overtones of the drum are brought out when the stroke is done correctly. The palm stroke is done by hitting the center of the drum with the flat palm. The touch is simply fingertip contact with the drumhead.

The slap is one of the most important strokes on the conga drum, and perhaps the hardest stroke for the student to master. While the slap can be performed with one hand alone, it is usually done in conjunction with the other hand muffling the head. The hand is in much the same position as the open tone with the thumb held alongside the other fingers throughout the stroke. The palm of the hand hits the edge of the head first. On impact, the hand is thrown downward and forward.

In the examples for conga drumming, I will use abbreviations for the strokes: O=open; M=muff; B=bass; P=palm; S=slap; and T=touch.

The strokes played by the right hand are indicated by notes on the top space; strokes played by the left hand, on the second space. *In no way should this notational set-up be construed to signify differences in pitch.* Above the notes are the abbreviations for the various conga drum sounds.

The Tumbao

The basic pattern for the conga drum in salsa is called tumbao, a term with several usages. The ostinato played by the tumbadora in rumba, and the patterns played by the bass which line up with the conga drum pattern are also called tumbao. The word, which is derived from the verb "tumbar," is defined as "to tumble, fell, knock down, throw down, heave down." In colloquial usage, it means "to inebriate, to overpower, stun."[7] A writer for *Latin New York* gives it another meaning:

> . . . one of those catch-all music phrases used to describe an orchestra's particular sound, beat, rhythm and, in Latin music, its sense of identity. El Gran Combo has a tumbao—a readily identifiable sound which distinguishes EGC from all known imitators.[8]

The tumbao is played in all tempos except for the bolero, the slow ballad style. When played on one drum, the tumbao is a one measure ostinato figure:

Ex. 4.1. *The tumbao.*

In a recording of a salsa group, the open tones are usually the only clearly audible sounds coming from the conga drum. The closed tones contribute to the even eighth note flow, which is duplicated by the maracas and the bongós in their own characteristic fashion. As indicated above, the open tones (O) usually occur on the last two eighth notes of the measure, but they can be substituted by a single quarter note, or by an eighth note rest followed by an eighth note. Malabe points out that slight variations are made in the tumbao so that it flows well with the piano part. For example, accented notes in the piano may be accompanied by slaps on the conga.

Nowadays, it is far more common for the conguero to play a pair of conga drums, and the tumbao is played somewhat differently.

Ex. 4.2. *Tumbao played on two drums.*

In the above example, the notes below the staff are played on the lower-pitched drum. The pattern is reversible: that is, it can begin with the second measure as well as the first. Note that the first measure in the above example is identical to the the tumbao figure for one conga drum. In many performances I have heard, the conga player strays from this basic two-measure figure. Occasionally, he or she may place the low tones in both measures. In another variant, the low tones are played only intermittently. Both Amira and Malabe agree that when the pattern in Ex. 4.2 is repeated consecutively without variance, the low tones on the second drum are supposed to go in the three part of the clave. In other words, in the 2–3 clave the low tones are played in the second measure, while in 3–2 clave they go in the first measure. Some drummers play the tumbao exactly the same for a fast tempo as for a slow tempo. Other drummers, most notably the great Cuban conguero Tata Guines, play the slap in the 3 part of the clave with the left hand instead of the right hand at fast tempos:

Ex. 4.3. *Alternate form of the tumbao.*

The Band and Folkloric Styles

Conga players do not necessarily play both popular music and folkloric music. According to Malabe and Amira, a different style of playing is needed for each genre. There are band specialists, such as Frankie Malabe, and there are folklore specialists, such as John Amira. A few players, such as Malabe, can play both styles. Malabe states:

> Folklore drummers cannot do dance music, and band drummers do not play folkloric music too well. It's like frustration. The folkore players would like to play the band style; the band-style players would like to play the folklore style. You can put both together. It's very tricky, but it can be done: when to hold back, when to pick up the tempos, when to sound a little busier. It's not easy to do it—unless the arranger is with you and says: "Let's write the arrangement around the drum."

Although the playing styles of congueros are strongly influenced by personal choices, we can enumerate a few distinctions between the folklore and band styles.

Band drummers favor the louder fiberglass-shell drums while folkloric drummers choose wooden drums. Soloing in folkloric style is sparse, while band soloing tends to be fuller. While folkloric drummers space their ideas, band congueros tend to run their ideas together in a display of technique.

The Timbales

The timbales is the term for a drum set composed of two single-skinned drums with a shell made of steel-reinforced stainless steel, plus a set (usually a pair) of suspended cowbells. In addition, many timbales players, known as timbaleros, add a suspended cymbal, and some use a woodblock. The timbalero plays in a standing position. The word "timbal" (singular of timbales) actually refers only to the drums; the English word is timpani, or kettle drums. The timbales used in Latin music were, in fact, devised as a smaller and less booming replacement for the kettle drums. Another name given to the drums is pailas. The widths of the heads are 13 inches and 14 inches, but wider drums are also used. In addition, there are smaller models known as timbalitos. The timbales are played with sticks, or by hand in one accompaniment style. The larger drum is placed to the left side. The cowbells are affixed to a stand between the two drums. There are usually a pair of cowbells of different sizes, with the smaller one, known as the cha cha bell, placed above the larger one, or mambo bell. The technique of the timbales is elaborate, and the timbalero in salsa often is required to perform some of the functions of a jazz drummer. Here I will touch on the most basic aspects of the instrument.

Playing Techniques

The playing technique encompasses three aspects: accompanying, soloing and playing breaks ("cierres"). A common accompaniment to singing and instrumental solos is for the right hand to play cowbell, wood-block or on the sides of the timbales. Meanwhile, the left hand plays on the second and fourth beats of every measure, usually without a stick. The left hand pattern consists of a muffled stroke followed by an open stroke created by a snap of the wrist. This pattern is played on the large timbal. The figure played by the right hand is known as cáscara (lit. "rind, shell"):

Ex. 4.4a. *Cáscara in 2–3 clave.*

Ex. 4.4b. *Cáscara in 3–2 clave.*

This figure (also called "paila") is typically played on the shell of the drums. At times, the timbalero plays on the shells of both drums simultaneously. Sheller marks "cáscara" in the timbales part when he wants the timbalero to play the figure. Malabe emphasizes the importance of maintaining the cáscara pattern without variance once it is started. He prefers the timbales player to pick up the cáscara pattern after a break figure, instead of, say, filling in the few beats with quarter notes; good players will play part of the ending of the pattern, then start the pattern again. In the two examples below, the first measure of each plus the quarter note rest in the second measure is the break fig-

GUITAR SHOWCASE

3090 So. Bascom Ave

San Jose, CA 95124

"Musician's Discount Headquarters"

1360 41st. Avenue

Capitola, CA 95010

SOLD BY		DATE
9050		4.14.94

SOLD TO Salsa Rythm

ADDRESS

CITY, STATE, ZIP | **PHONE**

ON ACCOUNT	PAID ACCOUNT	RESALE	FINANCE	C.O.D.

WARRANTY ☐ 30 DAY STORE ☐ 90 DAY FACTORY ☐ 1 YEAR FACTORY

CREDIT CARD	PAID OUT	CASH	#	CHECK NO.

QUAN	COMPUTER #	DESCRIPTION	UNIT PRICE	AMOUNT
1	4195510	Salsa.		12.95
			#	1.07
				$14.02

HEARD ABOUT US FROM: ☐ 1-RADIO _____ ☐ 6-SHOWCASE TIMES ☐ 7-BAM
☐ 8-GOODTIMES ☐ 9-MICRO TIMES ☐ 10-TV. _____ ☐ 15-PAPER ☐ 16-YELLOWPAGE
☐ 17-OTHER:

RECEIVED BY   **THANK YOU**

364467

ure, which all the percussion instruments play together. In Ex. 4.5a the player fills in the second measure with quarter notes; in Ex. 4.5b, he or she comes out of it with the last three beats of the cáscara figure, as Malabe prefers:

Ex. 4.5a. *Break figure followed by quarter notes.*

Ex. 4.5b. *Break figure followed by remainder of cáscara.*

Another timbales technique is a pick-up phrase known as the "abanico," which is typically played in the last measure of a break. The figure consists of a rimshot on the third beat, followed by a roll on the fourth beat concluding on the first beat of the following measure.

In dance styles related to salsa, the timbales is assigned other patterns besides the cáscara. In the danzón, a dance rhythm dating back to the last half of the nineteenth century, the timbales plays a five-stroke rhythm known as cinquillo:

Ex. 4.6a. *Cinquillo.*

Several authorities[9] have called the cinquillo the rhythmic base of Cuban music, but its presence in salsa is limited to a derivative rhythm, known as tresillo, which appears in bass figures:

Ex. 4.6b. *Tresillo.*

Another figure is the baqueteo, a two-measure pattern consisting of a steady stream of eighth notes played alternatively on various parts of the two timbales drums. Humberto Morales states that the player "is actually trying to imitate the sound of the bongos."[10] The baqueteo is not played in salsa; it was popular before the 1950s.

As I have already suggested, the timbales have a long history. It begins in the eighteenth century in an ensemble known as orquesta típica ("typical orchestra"). The instrumentation included woodwinds and brass instruments, a few strings; the Creole kettle drums were in the percussion section along with the güiro. Around the end of the nineteenth century, a new ensemble emerged: the charanga francesa, now known simply as charanga ("French military band" is one possible translation.)[11] It was composed of a wooden flute, piano, bass, violins, güiro and the timbales, a small version of the kettle drums. In the 1940s, timbaleros such as Tito Puente adopted a "hotter" style of playing which showed the influence of rumba: the soloing was based on quinto soloing, and the cáscara pattern was taken from the rumba accompaniment figure played on a woodblock by "palitos" ("little sticks"). Originally, bands would combine the conga drum with the bongós or the timbales, but not usually both. Since the advent of salsa, however, the percussion trio of timbales, bongós and congas has become standard. In the bands patterned after the conjunto sound of the 1940s, timbales are not usually used.

The Bongós

The bongós are an instrument of Cuban origin consisting of two drums joined together. The large head is called "hembra" (female); the small head, "macho" (male). The heads, which are made of calfskin, are approximately 7 ¼ inches and 8 ½ inches. The instrument is customarily played between the player's legs while he or she is seated. The large head is on the right side of the player. The bongós are tuned to a high pitch, as they are noted for their sharp, cutting timbre.

The basic rhythm of the bongós is called martillo ("hammer"), which consists of a steady eighth note pattern in which the hands alternate: right, left, right, left. Beats 1, 2, 3, and 4 are stressed, and produce a hammer-like sound. Beats 1 and 3 are further accented by raising the pitch of the small drum. This effect is created by pressing in the center of the drum head with the thumb of the left hand and simultaneously striking the same drum with the index finger. Beat two has an open stroke on the small drum; beat four, one on the large drum. The strokes on the off-beats are produced by all finger tips together, or with the side of the thumb. In some variations the stroke on the "and" after four is accented instead of on the first beat. With the exception of the martillo, all strokes are done by the index fingers which produce a sharp sound.[12]

In general, the bongosero is allowed greater improvisatory freedom than the other members of the percussion section while accompanying vocal or instrumental features. The soloing is strongly reminiscent of the quinto drum in rumba. Often, phrases played on the large drum are answered by the small drum. This finds its parallel in quinto playing with its alternations between slaps and open tones.

In the son groups, also called agrupaciónes, the bongós were the main percussion instrument, and were unaccompanied by conga or timbales. Without the underpinning of the conga's tumbao, the bongós have a more dominant sound, and the bongoseros in the son groups were improvising in a more aggressive fashion behind the rest of the group. The sound quality and technique differed from the current practice. The larger drum, and possibly the smaller one as well, was tuned to a lower pitch. Most prominent of all the bongó techniques was a finger roll, an effect now associated only with the conga drum and called a "moose" because of the similarity of the sound it produces to a moose call. The finger roll is produced by rubbing a finger braced by a thumb across the head, which must be rather loose for the sound to be produced.[13]

In salsa groups, the bongosero switches to the hand-held cowbell, known as campana, during the montuno section. If the arrangement calls for a piano solo during this section, the bongosero will usually put down the campana and return to the bongós.

The Cowbell

The introduction of the hand cowbell and the use of it on a regular basis is attributed to Arsenio Rodriguez. The bongosero holds the cowbell in the left hand with the rim or open part of the bell facing away from the player. A hammer shaft is used as a beater. Strokes are played over the rim or near the closed end, producing a strong, low sound and a high, weak sound respectively. Some bells have a raised indentation in the middle, and the player can place strokes on either side of the ridge in addition to the rim and closed end, producing additional tonal effects. In the notated examples below the low sound is placed on the second space; the high sound, on the top space. All strokes can be muted, but the strokes played near the closed end are usually muted by the left hand index finger on the back of the bell. This muting action is perceived by its executant as part of the pattern. The current pattern is:

Ex. 4.7a. *Bell pattern in 2–3 clave.*

Ex. 4.7b. *Bell pattern in 3–2 clave.*

In Cuba, according to Malabe, they sometimes do only the first measure of the hand cowbell pattern, omitting the second measure entirely:

Ex. 4.8. *Alternate bell pattern.*

For the playing technique of the maracas, claves, güiro and vibra-slap, an excellent source is Birger Sulsbrück's *Latin American Percussion: Rhythms and Rhythm Instruments from Cuba and Brazil.*[14]

PART II

Other Genres
Related to Salsa

Chapter Five

The Music of Santería

The music and instruments of the Santería religion have had a pervasive influence on salsa. Many salsa musicians are Santeros—people who have been initiated into the religion. Santería is based on the beliefs of the Yoruba people of Nigeria and the worship of Yoruba deities known as orishas.[1] It originated in Cuba among the Yoruba slaves, who were known as Lucumí.[2] Since the late 1960s, the religion has gained many adherents in New York and Miami. The growth of the religion in the United States stemmed from two important developments: the Cuban immigration after Castro's rise to power and the embrace of Yoruba culture by many American blacks.[3]

Santería chants, which are sung in the Yoruba language, have been performed by a number of prominent musicians including Celia Cruz, Mongo Santamaria, Arsenio Rodriguez, Milton Cardona, Julito Collazo and Daniel Ponce. Like salsa, many of these chants feature a call-and-response interchange between a lead singer and a coro (chorus).

The Batá Drums

The batá drums are the principle and most important drums of Santería. Like the religion, the drums came to Cuba with the Yoruba slaves; today, they are still performed for religious rituals in Nigeria. The function of the batá drums is to talk to the orishas and call them down to their respective devotees. Their rhythms are based on a drum language which reproduces the tonal changes and speech patterns of the Yoruba language. The drums may be played alone, or they may accompany the chants.

Since the early 1970s, the batá drum ensemble has found a home for itself in the more experimental salsa groups. Groups which have used the batá drums include the Cuban group Irakere, Jerry Gonzalez' Fort Apache Band, the Puerto Rican group Batacumbele led by percussionist "Cachete" Maldonado, and Zaperoko, co-led by the late Frankie Rodriguez and Edwin Feliciano.

The batá drums are dual-headed, hour-glass shaped drums which come in three sizes: the iyá (often called caja in New York), the itótele and the okónkolo (also called kónkolo, oméle or améle). The batá drums come closer to having a fixed pitch than any other Afro-Cuban percussion instrument. The drums are placed on the laps of the seated drummers so that the drum heads face out on either side. Both heads are played. The large head of each drum is called énu (Yoruba for "mouth"); the small head, tcha tchá ("anus"). All three batá drums are invariably performed together as an ensemble. Each drum is played by one musician. A batá player is called an olubatá, and the olubatá who plays the iyá is called kpuátaki.[4] In Spanish, the drummers are known as tamboleros or bataleros; only men may play batá.

The largest drum is the iyá (Yoruba for "mother") and is played by the leader of the batá ensemble. It has the most prominent solo role and also supplies cues to the other drummers. Attached to the border of the iyá's skins is a string of small bells called ichauoró or chaguoro. The itótele is the middle drum and closely follows the lead of the iyá. The smallest drum in the ensemble is the okónkolo. It is assigned short ostinato phrases and requires the least amount of expertise of the three. Traditionally, the beginning batalero learns the okónkolo, proceeds to the itótele and finally learns the iyá.

Types of Batá Drum Phrases

Bataleros must practice and memorize numerous rhythmic patterns known as toques. These toques are not improvised; each is associated with a specific orisha, and must be played in a specific tempo and dynamic range. Amira states:

> With every rhythm that is specifically tied to an orisha, you try
> to capture the essence of the orisha. First of all, the rhythm
> stays in a fixed form; they already contain the essence of the
> orisha. Each one has built into it something that gives you a cer-
> tain feeling when you listen to it.

In addition, the bataleros must learn three types of phrases: conversaciónes (conversations), llames (calls) and viros.

Conversaciónes

The iyá player plays certain phrases in which he is said to be talking
with the orisha. The sounds he produces are a re-creation in drum language of the tonal aspects of Yoruba. He plays these conversaciónes
(also called lenguas in Cuba) between two toques, or in the middle of
a toque. In some instances, he substitutes these phrases for an entire
toque. Meanwhile, the okónkolo continues to play the basic rhythm of
the toque.[5]

Photograph courtesy of John Amira.

John Amira (left) performing with batá ensemble.

Llames

The llames (calls) are played by the iyá as a cueing device for the two other drums. Some llames are only a few beats long, while others are much longer. For each llame there is an appropriate response, or "respuesto." The llames are played at the start of each toque, or in the middle of one to indicate the start of another pattern or of a conversación. The llames, like the conversaciónes, occur at precise points in the ritual or in the development of the music, not at the whim of the player.[6]

Viros

While in some songs, the same rhythmic pattern is played throughout, others have various successive rhythms, and the pass from one to the other is called "vuelta" or "viro." At times, the viros can occur when the dancers are protraying a different attribute of an orisha. For example, in one dance to Changó, one viro occurs when the dancers are evoking thunder, an attribute of Changó; another, when the masculine prowess of Changó is being portrayed, and so on.[7]

Clave in Batá

The concept of clave is at the root of batá drumming. Musicians base the starting points for their parts in a particular toque by its relation with the clave pattern, and the length of the part is judged by how long it takes for the part to be synchronized with the start of the clave, or how many repetitions before it lines up again with the start of the clave. In a few toques, the clave is not strictly adhered to. Amira states that in one instance, the iyá and itótele repeat a pattern that is only seven beats long; in another toque, the iyá plays a long conversation which ends a beat short. But these are exceptions to the rule.

The chants and batá patterns of Santería comprise a large body of work which has not been brought to the attention of the public outside of Latin neighborhoods. The music has influenced many salsa musicians, who have made a practice of including the music of Santería in public performances alongside more popular material.

Chapter Six

La Rumba

Rumba is a sort of Afro-Cuban party music which incorporates percussion, dancing and commentary on everyday life. Unlike the batá, the rumba developed in a secular context. Originally, ordinary objects such as frying pans, spoons, the backs of chairs, cabinet drawers and crates carried the rhythm. The word rumba typically refers to street music performed by percussion and voices in parks and street corners. People who perform the music are called "rumberos," and they are said to be having a "rumbon." In New York, these rumbones have taken place all over the city, including Central Park, and were the training grounds for New York salsa percussionists since the late 1940s.[1] The folkloric rumba, which has had a profound effect on salsa, in no way resembles the Cuban songs popular in the United States in the 1930s (such as "The Peanut Vendor") which Americans called rhumba. At the time, all Cuban music in the United States was called "rhumba," and the groups which performed the music were likewise called "rhumba orchestras." Unlike the folkloric rumba, rhumba was not very involved rhythmically, and it was easily adapted to ballroom dancing. Some musicians in Cuba and the United States give the latter the name "rhumba with an H" to distinguish it from the rhythmically volatile and percussive music.[2]

There are three main types of rumba: guaguancó, rumba columbia, and yambú. Presently, the guaguancó and the rumba columbia are performed using all three members of the conga drum family: the tumbadora (the largest conga drum), the segunda (the middle drum) and the quinto (smallest size). The guaguancó has been performed on the conga drums at least since the 1930s.[3] The yambú is most characteristically performed on packing crates. The percussionists do not usually sing.

The guaguancó, yambú and rumba columbia are distinguished from each other by different rhythms, tempos, meters, text styles and choreography. What they have in common is the alternation of a lead singer and a chorus, an attribute shared by many musics of African descent, and a form in which the lead singer first sings alone and then in a call-and-response with the chorus. The first part of the text which is sung solo is called "el canto," while the second part is called "el montuno." In Cuba, the lead singer is called "el gallo" and the chorus, "el vasallo."[4] In all three types, the highest drum, whether it is a quinto or the smallest packing crate in the group, is the lead, soloing drum, and it responds to the movements of the dancers, or vice-versa, while the other drums play a decidedly accompanying role. In addition, they all share the use of palitos, or "little sticks," (also used in the non-diminutive form—"los palos") which play on a woodblock or any wooden surface such as the side of a conga drum. The palitos play basically the same pattern for all three rumba styles. A singing member of the ensemble frequently plays the claves. All of the following examples of rumba playing were taught to me by John Amira.

Guaguancó

The guaguancó is a couple dance in a medium to fast tempo which pantomimes the man's efforts to seduce a woman and her repulsion of the man. If the man's efforts are successful, the dance climaxes in an activity known as "vacunar" and an act called "el vacunao." The pelvic thrusts done by the man in the vacunao symbolize the sexual act. According to one interpretation, the dance is "a pantomime of the courtship between the rooster and the chicken with convulsive-like gestures in rhythm with the quinto drum."[5] Like the conga drums, the vacunao has its roots in Congolese culture; it comes from the fertility dance known as yuka.[6]

The text of the guaguancó deals with commentary on everyday life; the phrase "la rumba buena" (the good rumba) is often sung, and there are probably other stock phrases. Arsenio Rodriguez once related to an interviewer the origin of the music:

It is said that it originated in Havana in the slums called "El Reverbero Caliente," "Los Cariñosos" and others, where groups of families and friends got together. The purpose of these meetings was not so much to entertain, but rather to discuss, to the beating of the claves and conga drums, the occurrences of infidelities between husband and wife, and at other times, of insults.[7]

One scholar notes that in times past, singers improvised the lyrics in décimas, a poetic form consisting of ten-line verses in rhymed octosyllables. The rhyme scheme is as follows: first line with the fourth and fifth; the second line with the third; the sixth line with the seventh and tenth; the eighth with the ninth.[8] The décima form is used in several Cuban and Puerto Rican musical idioms.

The guaguancó often opens with a section called "la Diana," in which the lead singer sings vocables. Then the singer proceeds to the text section (el canto) and the call-and-response section (montuno).

Claves and Palitos Patterns

There are several different styles of playing guaguancó; perhaps the most influential are the Havana and the Matanzas styles. They differ in the patterns played by the conga drums only; the same patterns are played by the claves and the palitos in both styles.

The claves customarily play a pattern called the guaguancó or rumba clave, which differs from the band-style or son clave because the third stroke falls a half-beat later:

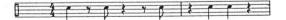

Ex. 6.1a. *Guaguancó clave.*

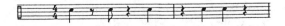

Ex. 6.1b. *The son clave.*

A less common claves pattern is:

Ex. 6.1c. *Alternate claves pattern.*

The palitos play a pattern without variation throughout the rumba. There are really two versions played; Ex. 6.2a is presently more common than Ex. 6.2b, according to John Amira. The notation reflects the sticking preferred by Amira, and does not reflect differences in pitches. Notes on the second space are played by the left stick; on the top space, by the right stick:

Ex. 6.2a. *Palitos pattern A for guaguancó.*

Ex. 6.2b. *Palitos pattern B for guaguancó.*

The sticking pattern in Ex. 6.2a brings out beats one and three; in Ex. 6.2b it emphasizes the strokes of the rumba clave (cf. Ex. 6.1a). Ex. 6.2b is the cáscara pattern; timbales players adopted this pattern from the palitos in guaguancó.

In notating the examples for conga drumming, I will use abbreviations for the strokes: O=open; M=muff; B=bass; P=palm; S=slap; and T=touch. Except where indicated otherwise, the strokes played by the right hand are indicated by notes on the top space; strokes played by the left hand, on the second space. *In no way should this notational set-up be construed to signify differences in pitch.* Above the notes are the abbreviations for the various conga drum sounds.

Havana Style

The Havana style of playing guaguancó is by far the most famous style. While the Matanzas style and the other styles of playing guaguancó are perhaps more at home in their original settings, the Havana style has become the standard way of playing. When one hears guaguancó on recordings made by salsa musicians, this is the style they are following. The distinguishing characteristic of the Havana style of guaguancó is a pattern which results when you combine the parts of the supporting drums of tumbadora and segunda parts, omitting all but the open tones:

Ex. 6.3. *Resultant pattern for guaguancó, Havana style.*

The pattern consists of low tones alternating with high tones, played respectively on the tumbadora and the segunda: notes on the second space in Ex. 6.3 are the tones of the tumbadora; on the top space, the tones of the segunda. The patterns continue with little divergence throughout the performance while the quinto drum improvises. The pattern is formed by the combination of the following two patterns:

Ex. 6.4a. *Segunda (middle drum) pattern for guaguancó, Havana style.*

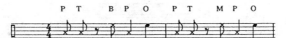

Ex. 6.4b. *Tumbadora (low drum) pattern for guaguancó, Havana style.*

The open tones seem to jump from one drum to the next in a conversation, and it gave me a thrill to hear the pattern emerge the first time I played it with Amira. While in the folkloric context the patterns are played by two congueros, each with his/her own drum, it is played by one conguero alone in a band setting using two drums:

Ex. 6.5a. *Guaguancó, Havana style, played by one conguero on two drums.*

In the above example, the notes below the full staff are played by the lower drum. Frankie Malabe sometimes uses the vocables "Ba-keem, ba-keem" to indicate the guaguancó pattern, because of the sound pattern in the circled area of Ex. 6.5b:

Ex. 6.5b. *Vocables for the guaguancó, Havana style.*

In recordings made in the last three decades, the patterns of the supporting drums as notated in Ex. 6.4a and Ex. 6.4b begin in either the three part or the two part of the clave. Starting the pattern on the three clave has a bizarre effect on the listener in terms of his perception of the clave: he hears the three part of the clave *followed* by a pattern rhythmically identical to the three part of the son clave pattern:

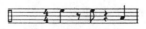

Ex. 6.6.
Three open tones in guaguancó, Havana style, following the open tone on the upbeat.

In other words, the phrase in Ex. 6.6 falls on the two part of the clave. For some reason, musicians never interpret this paradoxical relation with the clave as being "cruzao," or starting a pattern on the wrong measure of the clave. Playing the guaguancó in this fashion yields a sort of call-and-response relation with the clave, and it enhances the rhythmic complexity of the performance. Actually, this arrangement vis-a-vis the clave presently is by far the more common one. Amira believes that the form in which the measure with the three open tones falls on the three part of the clave might have been more popular before the 1950s. Malabe thinks that the two ways of fitting with the clave may have originally reflected regional differences of playing within Cuba.

Matanzas Style

The Matanzas style has three open tones where the Havana style has four. In addition, the rhythms are meant to be played in an uneven rhythm. The resultant pattern formed by the interlocking of the open tones of the segunda and the tumbadora is as follows:

Ex. 6.7. *Resultant pattern for guaguancó, Matanzas style.*

The pattern consists of low tones alternating with high tones, played respectively on the tumbadora and the segunda: notes on the second space in Ex. 6.7 are the tones of the tumbadora; on the top space, the tones of the segunda. The pattern is formed by the combination of the following two patterns:

Ex. 6. 8a. *Segunda part for guaguancó, Matanzas style.*

Ex. 6.8b. *Tumbadora part for guaguancó, Matanzas style.*

In both the tumbadora and segunda parts in the Matanzas style, the first stroke is actually slightly shorter than a quarter note. All the rest of the strokes are then shifted back. Although the actual sound of this style is uneven, I chose to use simpler rhythmic values such as quarter notes and eighth notes rather than attempt to represent it using combinations of 32nd notes, etc. In comparison, the Havana style is rhythmically even, and it can be notated with rhythmic values of eighth and quarter notes producing a faithful representation of the actual sound quality.

One of the features of the style is the freedom which it affords the supporting drums to stray from their respective ostinato patterns. Because of the absence of the third open tone, there is more room to fill in, according to Amira:

> By the fact that they have that single tone on the segunda [see
> Ex. 6.8a], it opens up areas of variation on the drum that you
> can't get with the Havana style. For example, there's a lot of
> conversation that can take place between the low drum and the
> middle drum.

The Matanzas style is played by one conguero on two drums as follows:

Ex. 6.9. *Guaguancó, Matanzas style, played on two drums.*

Rumba Columbia

The rumba columbia is the most African sounding of the three types of rumba, and it differs from the guaguancó and the yambú in several respects. It is in a very fast $^6_8$, and is danced by a solo male dancer rather than a couple. It is said to have developed in rural Matanzas.[9] Unlike the other types of rumba, the text is largely in African dialects. According to one source, the text makes "references (usually joking or satirical) to the Lucumí and Abakwá rituals. The soloist often gets into a rhythmic 'argument' with the lead drummer."[10]

Claves and Palitos Patterns

The claves pattern in rumba columbia is a $^6_8$ version of the guaguancó pattern; the sound of the $^6_8$ clave in rumba columbia is close in sound to the $^4_4$ rumba clave pattern. In fact, many of the patterns used in rumba columbia sound like they are in $^4_4$.

Ex. 6.10. $^6_8$ *claves pattern for rumba columbia.*

The palitos parts are as follows:

Ex. 6.11a. *Palitos pattern A for rumba columbia.*

Ex. 6.11b. *Palitos pattern B for rumba columbia.*

Ex. 6.11a is basically the same as Ex. 6.2a; and Ex. 6.11b, as Ex. 6.2b. Ex. 6.11a—like Ex. 6.2a—has become the more common form.

Conga Patterns

There are several different supporting drum patterns, but the resultant pattern in the example below is the most common:

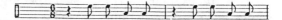

Ex. 6.12.

Resultant pattern of open tones played by segunda (top space) and tumbadora (second space) for rumba columbia.

The pattern is formed by the combination of the following two patterns:

Ex. 6.13a. *Segunda part for rumba columbia.*

Ex. 6.13b. *Tumbadora part for rumba columbia.*

In another mode of playing rumba columbia, the performance begins as in Ex. 6.12 but eventually changes to the following resultant pattern:

Ex. 6.14.

Alternate resultant pattern of open tones played by segunda (top space) and tumbadora (second space) for rumba columbia.

Yambú

The yambú, like the guaguancó, is a couple dance in $^4_4$ with Spanish lyrics. The tempo is somewhat slower than the guaguancó. It also begins with a la Diana section of vocables before proceeding on to the text. The yambú follows a verse form known as regina, a form of traditional Spanish poetry consisting of four-line stanzas.[11] The dancing is slower, and is said to be imitating the movements of old people. There is no vacunao. The yambú is performed on two packing crates with the accompaniment of a bottle struck by a coin. The types of crates to be used have been prescribed over the years, with the quinto role played on a little crate formerly used for candles, and the tumbadora role played on a crate for the dried codfish popular in the Caribbean with the Spanish name "bacalao."[12] Amira told me that Eloy Martí, a Cuban percussionist, claimed to have been in the first group in Havana to play the yambú, and that it arose out of one of the periods when drums were confiscated by the authorities.

The rumba, like the music of Santería, came from slaves of African descent and their descendants. It is music designed for spontaneous street performances rather than for dance halls, nightclubs and the concert hall. When professional musicians played the rumba, they gave it a more polished sound, even adding instruments not traditionally associated with it.

As we shall see in the next chapter, the danzón and son also had a strong influence on salsa. They were far more popular than the rumba, and attracted a broad audience in Cuba and abroad. The danzón and son groups typically performed in professional music venues, and their music reflected a strong European influence.

Chapter Seven

El Danzón y
El Son

The danzón and the son are the direct forerunners of salsa. The danzón evolved into the mambo and the cha cha chá, dance rhythms which became famous in Latin music in the 1940s and 1950s. The son had all the qualities of salsa: an emphasis on Cuban percussion instruments, the use of a call-and-response section called montuno and a lead singer who improvised his or her text.

El Danzón

The danzón evolved from the French contredanse. The contredanse came to Cuba in the hands of the slaves and colonists who immigrated from Santo Domingo during the slave uprising of 1791 and settled in Oriente, the easternmost province in Cuba. The contradanza, a line dance in two repeated sections, was in a fast $^2_4$ tempo. From the contradanza evolved the danza, the habanera, the tango and the danzón. The name danzón is believed to be a composite of danza and son; as time went on, the influence of the son on the danzón increased.[1] Until the turn of the century, the contradanza and its descendants were played by an ensemble known as "orquesta típica," a cornet-led group with brass, woodwinds, strings, güiro and a Creole tympani. One standard instrumentation was: two clarinets, three brass, two violins, one string bass, two tympani and güiro.[2]

The first danzón, "Las Alturas de Simpson," was composed in 1879 by Miguel Failde (1848–1921). A native of Matanzas, Failde is regarded as the Father of the danzón. What distinguishes the danzón from its predecessors, besides the addition of a third section, was the increased use of the cinquillo rhythm:

Ex. 7.1. *Cinquillo.*

The cinquillo rhythm occurs in the melody and in the tympani accompaniment; scarcely a measure goes by where it is not played in one part or another. The dance style was less rigid and formal than in the contradanza; it eventually developed into a couple dance under the influence of the son.[3]

All of the following developments in the history of the danzón were associated with a new type of ensemble which developed at the turn of the century called charanga francesa, or simply charanga. The instrumentation included a few violins, string bass, the Cuban wooden flute, güiro and timbales, a smaller version of the Creole tympani with a less booming sound. After a few years, composer-pianist Antonio Maria Romeu established the piano as a regular member of the ensemble. The development of the new ensemble came about in part because the upper classes wanted a quieter, more genteel performance of the danzón for their indoor events, and the charanga groups soon were hired to perform in the homes, clubs and literary societies of the wealthy.[4]

The orquesta típica continued to be in existence until about 1916; until its demise, the danzón was performed outside by this ensemble and indoors by the charanga.[5] The charangas played in a more restrained and "professional" manner than the orquestas típicas, whose sound is reminiscent of the early New Orleans jazz bands.[6]

The Danzón con Montuno and the Danzonete

The new developments of the danzón were largely a result of the influence of the son. The most basic change came with the addition of the montuno, which was quickly established as the final section of the danzón. José Urfé's "El Bombín de Barreto," written in 1910, added two new sections to the danzón. The last section, called montuno, featured cornet and, in future danzónes, an improvised piano solo of indeterminate length. This new style was called danzón con montuno.

In 1929, Aniceto Díaz wrote "Rompiendo la Rutina" ("Breaking the Routine"). With this piece, a style which Díaz called danzónete, the composer introduced singing for the first time into the danzón. Formerly, the danzón was known as a purely instrumental form, while the son featured singing. Another influence of the son in the performance of the piece was the inclusion of claves and maracas.[7]

The Mambo and the Cha Cha Chá

With the development of the mambo (the Cuban name for Congolese-derived chants) the danzón's immersion into the Afro-Cuban heritage was complete.[8] The mambo first entered the danzón in a piece called "Mambo" written in 1938 by Orestes Lopez. Lopez was a member of a seminal group in Latin music, Arcaño y sus Maravillas, led by flutist Antonio Arcaño. Arcaño had augmented the string section with a cello and a viola, and Lopez was the cellist in the group. Lopez and his brother, bassist Israel "Cachao" Lopez, were largely responsible for the repertoire of the group.

The mambo was based on the addition of a conga drum to Arcaño's group, an important innovation in the charanga instrumentation. The tumbao of the conga along with Cachao's rhythmic bass style provided the backbone of the new style, which was first simply called danzón de nuevo ritmo (danzón of the new rhythm) and then mambo. In the last part, or montuno, the violins played repeated phrases called guajeos in a rhythmic counterpoint to the tumbao, and above them both soared Arcaño's flute. Another innovation copied by all future timbaleros was the addition of a cowbell to the timbales set, played by Ulpiano Díaz in Arcaño's group. Jésus Perez, the pianist in the group, was one of the major influences on pianists of the next few decades, according to Oscar Hernández. Arcaño's success with the mambo had social repercussions, insofar as it led the lower classes to reclaim the danzón from the elite.[9] The group became popular in dance-halls and on the radio, and drove Arcaño y sus Maravillas to the crest of popularity in Cuba. In the 1940s, their only rival was Arsenio Rodriguez.[10]

Over a decade later, the Cuban pianist and arranger Perez Prado (also called Dámaso Perez Prado) used the term "mambo" for his own music, which was written for a jazz big band with a Latin rhythm section. His music featured contrasting riffs between the saxophones and the trumpets against a guajeo background. It was in a faster tempo than Arcaño's mambos. Prado made the mambo a single, independent entity, rather than a section of an arrangement. Prado's style became very popular after he established himself in Mexico, and its main features were adopted by the "Big Three" mambo bands of New York: Machito y sus Afro-Cubanos, Tito Puente and Tito Rodriguez.

The cha cha chá was an outgrowth of the danzón mambo. The first piece in the dance rhythm was "La Engañadora," written in 1951 by violinist Enrique Jorrín, a former member of Arcaño's group. The dance itself was not devised until the early 1950s.[11] The name cha cha chá came from the sound produced by the dancers' sliding feet. Using the charanga instrumentation as devised by Arcaño—strings, flute, bass, güiro, timbales and conga drum—Jorrín's piece called for unison singing from the members of the charanga in the second section of the danzón. The cha cha chá uses a four-square rhythm that is less syncopated than the mambo, and it has a "sweet" rather than "hot" feeling. The noted art historian Robert Farris Thompson, who has also written about Latin music, shows his preference for the rhythmically more syncopated music that came before and after the cha cha chá:

> [Jorrín] shattered the formal structure of the danzón, down to a
> rejection of its famous rhythmic module, the cinquillo. In its
> place he built an airy form of danzón-tinged music distin-
> guished by a unison chorus of vocalists (breaking a tradition of
> duos, to say nothing of bypassing West African call-and-
> response) and a most determined avoidance of the off-beat
> melodic phrasing so prized by the mamboists. It was a Creole
> regression and infinitely easier to dance than mambo.[12]

The groups which most popularized the cha cha chá in the early 1950s were Orquesta Aragón and flutist José Fajardo's groups. The development of the cha cha chá coincided with the birth of the LP record and the emergence of television, and these new forms of communication aided in establishing its popularity.[13]

In many arrangements, the cha cha chá concludes in a mambo tempo twice as fast as the beginning; the new section is marked "ritmo doble."

Son

The son was based on a combination of guitars and percussion instruments. As its fame spread, the son brought into public consciousness the instruments of Black Cuba, which previously had been confined to the slums. The compositions performed by son groups (also called agrupaciónes) begin with a short section called the largo, in which the lyrics are pre-arranged, followed by the montuno. The montuno (also called capetillo) has a call-and-response interchange between a chorus and one or more lead singers, known as sonero. In the pre-World War I son groups the improvised text in this section, called the soneo, often contained insulting double-entendres.

> With cryptic lyrics a sonero would question someone's intelligence, a woman's fidelity, a daughter's virginity, a man's clothes, his facial attractiveness, and many other words which would elicit a glare of hatred. This duel of lyrics would continue until one sonero would utter something so humiliating that 'una bronca' (a riot) would ensue. Whenever El Son was played, broncas always ensued.[14]

When the son became popular and the musicians developed aspirations of success, the soneros avoided the insults which gave the son a bad reputation.

The son began in Oriente province, the mountainous eastern-most part of the Cuban island. The son eventually made its way to Havana in 1916 largely because of a few musicians in the Permanente, as the armed forces were known in Cuba.[15] Within the Permanente was a group called Trio Oriental which, after a series of changes in membership and instrumentation became known in the 1920s as the Sexteto Habanero, one of the most famous son groups.[16]

The Sexteto and the Septeto

The Sexteto Habanero quickly popularized the son in Cuba and throughout Spanish-speaking communities abroad. The group established the sextet instrumentation: tres, guitar, string bass, bongós, maracas and claves. All the musicians sang except the bongosero.

The lead instrument was the tres, a guitar-like instrument of Cuban origin with three groups of doubled or tripled strings. It is played with a plectrum. Some tres players prefer to use guitars which have been converted into tres instruments by changing the chording and tuning.[17]

The use of the string bass was an innovation. Formerly, the bass lines were played by the botija, a clay jug tuned by filling it with varying amounts of water, or the marimbula, a large African-derived finger piano.

In 1927, several groups added a cornet or trumpet to the standard six instruments, and they were known as septetos. The Sexteto Habanero was one of the first groups to add the instrument, although they did not always record with it. Their most famous trumpet player was Felix Chapottin (1909–1982), who reached greater fame as a member of Arsenio Rodriguez' group.[18]

Ignacio Piñeiro (1886–1969) was one of the most famous son composers. In 1927 he founded the Septeto Nacional, which along with the Sexteto Habanero was one of the most famous groups of the 1920s and 1930s. He wrote songs inspired by guajira (Cuban peasant) music, as well as songs inspired by Afro-Hispanic cult music. His song, "Echale Salsita" is often cited as an early use of the word 'salsa' in a musical context. It was used by George Gershwin his Cuban Overture.[19]

Arsenio Rodriguez and the Son Conjunto

In the late 1930s, the instrumentation for the son changed into a format called the son conjunto. The solo trumpet was augmented by a second and then a third trumpet, and the piano joined the ensemble. With the additional instrumentation, arrangers came to be a necessity. The artists who led these changes included Arsenio Rodriguez, Eliseo Silveira and Niño Rivera.

Arsenio Rodriguez was born in Matanzas Province in Cuba in 1911, the same part of Cuba that gave the world the rumba columbia and the danzón. He is credited with introducing the conga drum and the hand-held campana (cowbell) into the ensemble. He popularized the dance rhythm known as son montuno, a mid-tempo, syncopated beat. Arsenio was blinded in his youth by a mule kick and was nicknamed "El Ciego Maravilloso" ("The Marvelous Blind Man"). He came to New York in the 1950s in order to have an operation to cure his blindness. The operation was unsuccessful, and he never returned to Cuba.

Although he was widely respected, he never attained a great level of popularity in New York. According to Malabe, his band had a tough, no nonsense way of performing the music, and people complained that they couldn't dance to it. Nevertheless, his conjunto sound had a profound effect on the salsa world.

Arsenio Rodriguez is noted for his compositions, many of which were later recorded by salsa artists, especially Larry Harlow and Eddie Palmieri. His lyrics reflected the concerns of a Black Cuban born of Congolese descent who was proud and knowledgeable about his African background. His sympathy for the cause of the international black struggle is expressed in "Aqui Como Allá" and "Vaya P'al Monte." Several of his songs make reference to Afro-Cuban music and rituals: "Chango Pachanga" is based on a Yoruba chant used in Santería, "Dundunbanza" is based on a ritual chant used in Palo, and "Yambú en Serenata" has many elements of the slow folkloric rumba dance known as yambú.

Summary

In the 1940s and 1950s, the mambo and the cha cha chá developed from the danzón and the son. Arrangers in Cuba and the United States enriched these dance styles with jazz harmonies. An increased interest in Afro-Cuban music developed, as demonstrated by the addition of the conga drum to rhythm sections.

Salsa represents a continuation of the above noted trends which developed out of the danzón and the son: the extensive use of jazz harmonies and Afro-Cuban idioms. Although salsa continues to be popular, a new genre has developed called songo.

Chapter Eight

Songo

In the last few years, a new dance rhythm has come to the fore called onda Areito or songo. Like most of the innovations in Latin music, it sprang from Cuba. The leading examples of the style are Los Van Van led by Juan Formell, and Orquesta Ritmo Oriental. Both of these groups are based on the traditional charanga instrumentation of strings, piano and percussion, but the bass and piano are electric. Orquesta Ritmo Oriental has a flute, the typical solo instrument in the charanga ensemble, while Formell balances his strings with trombones.

What differentiates this music from American salsa, among other less easy to describe attributes, is the successful integration of the drum set into Latin music. Malabe believes that the rhythm was created by Changuito, a percussionist with Los Van Van, and that it is close to twenty years old. The style of playing is based on the figures played on the timbales, which, in turn, were adapted from the segunda and palitos patterns used in rumba. In essence, the new Cuban drummers are playing rumba on the trap set. When a trap set is not played, the timbales player supplements his setup with the floor bass drum used in trap sets. Playing with the trap set player in the rhythm section is a conguero who usually plays a trio of conga drums. The patterns he or she plays involve more open tones than are used in the tumbao figure (See Ex. 4.2). According to Malabe, the bongós are rarely used when songo is being played. As a result of the preponderance of open tones and the absence of the bongós, the conga sound is more prominent than in salsa.

The songo was taken up by several groups outside of Cuba, most notably by the Puerto Rican groups, Batacumbele and Zaperoko. Their sound tends to be more experimental and jazz-oriented than that of their Cuban counterparts. Los Van Van, in particular, is obviously heading towards a more commercial sound with its use of drum machines on a recent album. Both Zaperoko and Batacumbele include the use of the batá on some selections, and show their fondness for Puerto Rican folkloric rhythms. Batacumbele is led by percussionist Angel "Cachete" Maldonado and features conguero Giovanni "Mañenguito" Hidalgo, who is considered one of the leading new stars on his instrument. Zaperoko was co-led by the late Frankie Rodriguez, who sang and played percussion on the albums.

Patterns Played in Songo

The main elements of the trap set include a cowbell stroke on every first and third beat and a bass drum stroke on the "and" after the second beat.

Trap set: space below staff = high hat, played with the foot; 1st space = bass drum; 2nd space = floor tom tom; 3rd space = snare; space above staff = mounted cowbell. Snare drum figures are played on the metal rim of the snare drum.

Ex. 8.1a. *Trap set part for songo in 3–2 clave.*

<u>Variants</u>
The tom-tom figures can be played on the snare, so that all the drum figures are played on that drum. The bass drum can be omitted entirely from the 2 part of the clave—the second measure of the above example. In this variant, the bass drum hits only on the bombo.

Photograph courtesy of Martin Cohen and Latin Percussion.™

Frankie Malabe.

Frankie Malabe created a four-measure songo pattern which he calls "Mala Songo." The snare drum notes are all rimshots:

Ex. 8.1b. *"Mala Songo" trap set part in 3–2 clave.*

Note the following: 1) The snare drum (third space) is playing the 3–2 rumba clave pattern throughout, except for the last two beats of the fourth and final measure; and 2) The resultant pattern formed by the strokes on the bass drum, snare, tom-tom and cowbell is similar to a palitos pattern in rumba (See Ex. 6.2a).

Conga Drum Parts

There really is no standard conga drum pattern used in songo, but on several recordings the conguero plays a sort of filled-in version of the rumba pattern (See Ex. 6.5a); the open tones are usually placed in the three part of the clave. The following is a pattern used in songo which matches up well with the trap set patterns in Ex. 8.1a and 8.1b:

Ex. 8.2. *Conga drum pattern for songo in 3–2 clave.*

C o n c l u s i o n

T his chapter begins with a review of the clave and a summary of the types of phrases played by the salsa rhythm section. Subsequent to this review is an analysis of salsa's characteristic traits.

Review

The Clave

The clave is the rhythmic formula *par excellence* of salsa. This two measure pattern is most typically performed on a pair of two round sticks known collectively as claves. The clave is embedded in the music whether or not it is actually stated; people who know the music well can hear it in the vocal lines, piano figures, horn parts and solos of a salsa arrangement. Tapping the clave from the beginning of a performance keeps one cognizant of its rhythmic center and enhances one's appreciation of the music. By finding the clave, the listener avoids getting lost in its rhythmic complications.

In addition to determining the nature of salsa, the clave is at the heart of the son, rumba and the music of Santería—Afro-Cuban idioms which have had a profound influence on salsa. It consists of five strokes: three strokes in the first measure and two strokes in the next. The measures of the clave are known respectively as the three part and the two part of the clave. The clave appears in $^4_4$ and $^6_8$.

In $^4_4$, two forms of the clave are used: the son clave and the rumba clave. They are differentiated by the placement of the third stroke, which falls on the last beat of the first measure in the son clave and a half beat later in the rumba clave. The $^6_8$ form of the clave is nearly indistinguishable from the rumba clave, although triplet values are used here instead of eighth notes.

A melody or performance can start with either the two part or the three part of the clave. When it begins with the three strokes, it is called 3–2 clave; beginning with the two strokes, it is 2–3 clave.

Types of Phrases in Salsa

The piano part consists of repeated phrases called guajeos which match up with the statements of the coro. In creating a guajeo, the pianist chooses between a "típica" (traditional) approach in which the left and right hands play an octave or a tenth apart, or a jazz approach using extended and/or altered harmonies.

The conguero and bongosero each play patterns consisting of a stream of eigthth notes. In both patterns, the musicians alternate between sounds created by striking various parts of the drum in different manners. The conga pattern is called tumbao; the bongó pattern, martillo ("hammer").

The bass part is not as easily categorizable as the other instruments. In many bass lines, the bassist anticipates the change in harmony; he or she consistently changes to the chord of the following measure on the fourth beat.

The timbales play a two-measure figure known as the cáscara. The pattern can begin on either of its two measures, and is usually played on the shells of the timbales drums. The cáscara comes from the rumba idiom, in which it is played by palitos.

The hand cowbell is played by the bongó player in the coro section. The cowbell, which is struck by a hammer shaft, has a two measure pattern which, like the cáscara and claves patterns, can begin on either of its two measures.

Salsa's Characteristic Traits

A salsa arrangement is composed of at least four sections: a verse, a montuno section based on a short series of repeated chord changes, an instrumental section called mambo with greater harmonic movement than in the montuno, and a return to the montuno. In addition, there may be other sections, depending on the arranger's decision. The sections are marked by clearly defined endings known as cierres, in which the members of the rhythm section (piano, bass and percussion instruments) play together in rhythmic unison. The weaving in and out of the montuno and the use of cierres to clearly define the ending of sections are two of the most identifiable traits of salsa.

Like other African-derived popular musical idioms, the music consists of a layering of ostinato figures. In salsa, each instrument plays its own characteristic pattern, especially in the open-ended montuno section of a salsa arrangement. These patterns are repeated with little or no variation.

In salsa, off-beat phrases are set against the backdrop of a steady stream of eighth notes. This stream of eighth notes is played by the conga drums, bongós and maracas in different patterns. The style of singing and instrumental performance is geared towards a rhythmic effect. Harmony also plays a role in creating rhythmic tension, with the voice, bass, piano and/or horns falling on harmonic downbeats at different points.

The lyrics of a salsa performance consist of the pre-arranged verse and statements of the coro, and the improvised "inspiraciónes" of the lead singer in the montuno section. A song begins with the development of a topic, which ends in an encapsulating short sentence. This sentence, which is sung in many repetitions by the coro, has the quality of a motto or slogan. The lead singer ("sonero") then creates his or her text by referring to or restating it. Thus on a purely textual level, salsa is characterized by the weaving in and out of a short, slogan-like sentence.

The interplay of innovation and tradition in salsa is a reflection of the Puerto Rican and Nuyorican musicians, who remain its greatest adherents. Although their music is based on dance rhythms originating in Cuba, they have put their own personal stamp on them. With the past as a guide, one can be safe in guessing that in salsa, Afro-Cuban authenticity will continue to blend with American popular idioms in new ways. We have written this book with the belief that learning about the components of salsa and related genres will help non-Hispanic listeners gain an "insider's" appreciation of the music.

Our approach has been musicological and based on transcriptions of live performances and recordings; we have tried to remain faithful to the nature of the music according to the perspective of its practitioners. We hope that we succeed in introducing listeners to this rhythmically compelling music.

Appendix A

Las Calles de Laredo

A Salsa Arrangement
by
Marty Sheller

In order to give an illustration of the form of a typical arrangement as well as other characteristics of salsa, we have included an arrangement by Marty Sheller of the folk song "Las Calles de Laredo" (The Streets of Laredo). Using a well-known song like "The Streets of Laredo" from a non-Hispanic culture is not unknown in Latin music; for example, Ray Barretto made a recording of "Greensleeves," and Cachao, an arrangement of "Ach Du Lieber Augustin."

Sheller and I decided to choose a melody sung in the United States in order to begin with material with which the reader may be familiar. This arrangement is somewhat shorter in spots than ones Sheller is asked to write, especially in the instrumental sections at letters D and H.

We have placed commentary below the music where it applies. The indications in the score itself are Sheller's alone.

Las Calles de Laredo

(The Streets of Laredo)

traditional

arranged by Marty Sheller

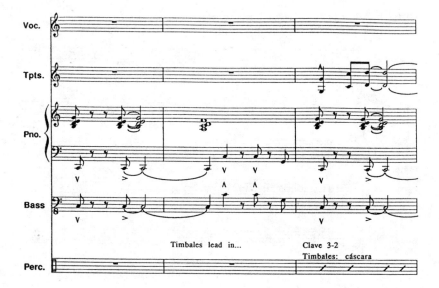

The Percussion Part

Most of the percussion part consists of indications to
the timbales player: where to play the cáscara figure
and various cymbal parts. Throughout the arrangement, Sheller indicates the clave to the percussionists
at several rehearsal letters.

Guía (A1 through A2)

Sheller changed the song from its original $^3_4$ meter to $^4_4$, and "felt" it as a 3–2 melody. I have omitted the English lyrics in the verse, since the song would sound more idiomatic if it were in Spanish.

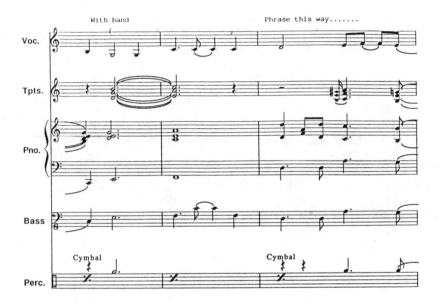

The Vocal Part

The vocal part is primarily a guide to the singer to add his or her own phrasing, except in A2, where Sheller indicates at one point that the singer has to hit a note "with the band" and in a subsequent measure to "Phrase this way."

Cierre

Sheller ends the guía with a cierre ("break"), in which
the full ensemble plays in rhythmic unison. The cierre
starts on the pick-up to the last measure of this page.

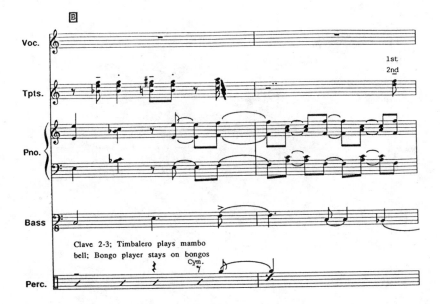

Shift from 3–2 clave to 2–3 clave

Because the previous section—A2—ended with a three measure phrase, B begins on the two part of the clave. The three trumpets play the coro melody at B for the first time, and then the singers take it up.

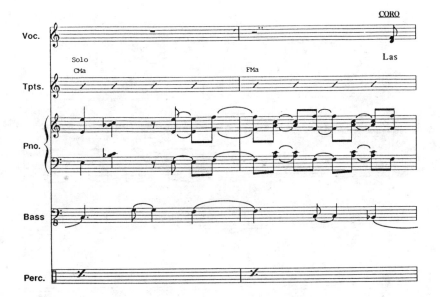

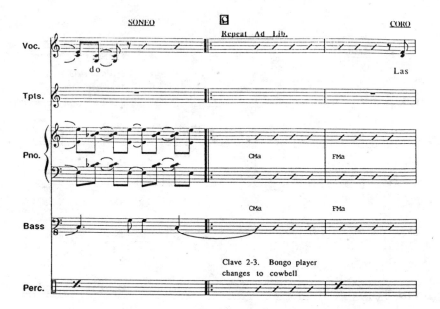

Coro Section

Letter C marks the start of the montuno. During this section, the piano plays a repeated pattern known as a guajeo or montuno. In this arrangement, the pianist can continue playing the four measure repeated phrase written out in B.

A coro (chorus) is sung over one complete statement of the guajeo. The coro is followed by the inspirations of the lead singer, also called the soneo. Sheller states that it is not at all uncommon for singers to write out a text for their inspirations when they are in the recording studio.

The end of the montuno (at letter D) is cued by the singer.

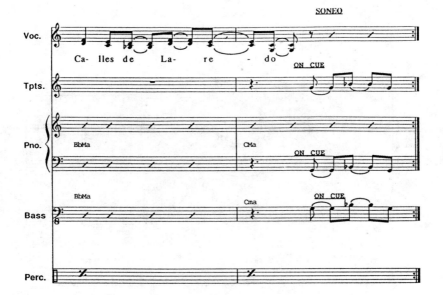

Mambo

Letter D marks the start of the mambo section, a feature for the instruments with no singing. Here, the arrangement typically is based on new harmonies different from those of the coro section. The reason that the section is called mambo is probably because it often contrasts a figure played in unison by the piano and bass with an entirely different figure played by the horns. The use of contrasting instrumental units, especially the saxophones against the trumpets, was a feature of the big bands popular in the 1950s, led by Perez Prado, Tito Puente and others, whose music was called "mambo."

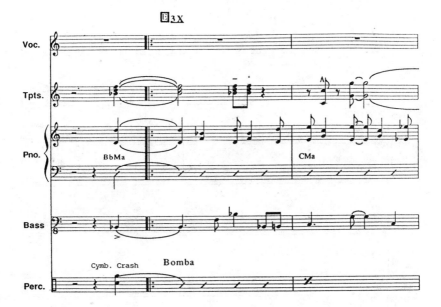

Bomba rhythm (E)

The bomba is a Puerto Rican folkloric rhythm, which salsa percussionists interpret using variants of the following cowbell and conga drum patterns:

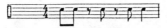

Cowbell pattern for bomba.

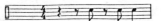

Conga drum pattern for bomba (open tones only).

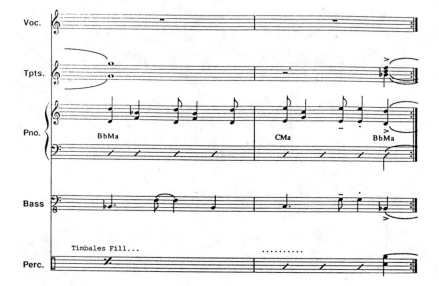

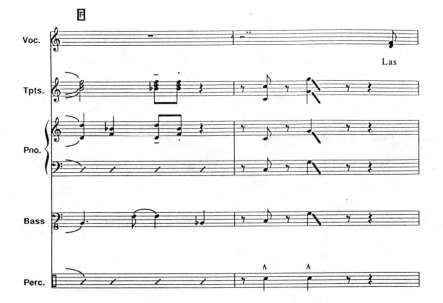

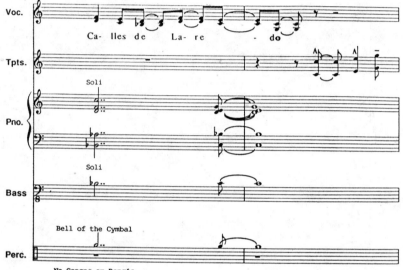

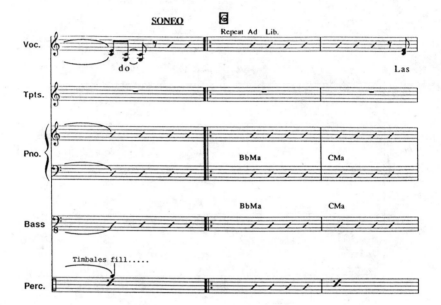

Second Coro Section (G)

In some variants, the original coro is truncated in the second coro section. Another variant is to reverse the order of coro-inspiration so that the inspiration comes first and the coro follows.

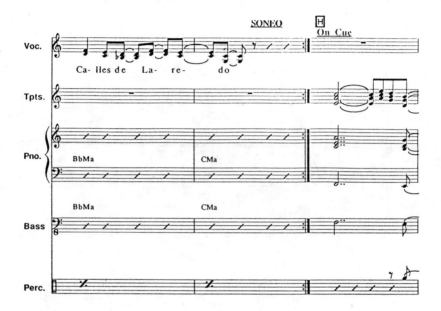

Moña Section

In some arrangements, an instrumental part known
as the moña follows the second coro section (see G).
Unlike the mambo section, the moña typically is based
on the same harmonies as the coro. However, H is a
simple instrumental introduction to the coda at I.

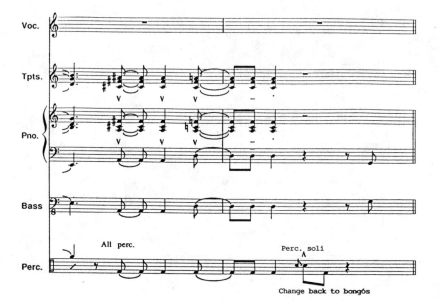

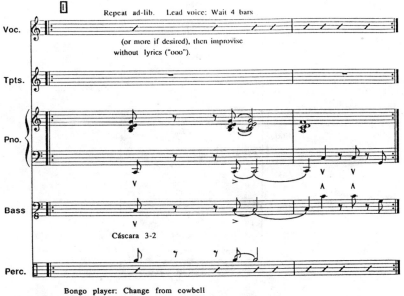

Coda

Because H is a three measure phrase, the coda begins on the three part of the clave. Note that the piano and bass figures are copied from the introductory section of the arrangement.

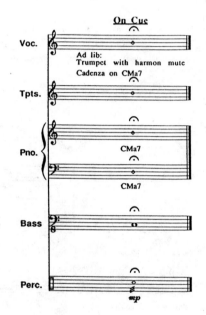

Appendix B

Canto a Chango

"Canto a Chango" ("Chant to Shango") is a song for the orisha Chango, the God of fire, thunder and lightning who is worshipped in the Santería religion. It is sung during Santería ceremonies—known as bembés—to call down the god and possess his acolytes.

This chant shares with salsa the call-and-response interplay between a coro and a lead singer. We have included it here to give an example of the music of Santería, which has grown to become a major influence on salsa. Many well-known artists have included the chants in their repertoire, and the sacred batá drums of Santería have been incorporated into the rhythm sections of several bands.

The music of "Canto a Chango" as it is presented here is based on a recording of Carlos "Patato" Valdez.* This chant has also been recorded by Celia Cruz, and by Arsenio Rodriguez with a slightly different melody. John Amira assisted in the transcription of the music and text.

* Carlos "Patato" Valdez, "Ready for Freddy," Latin Percussion-Ventures LPV–419 (1976).

Canto a Chango

I Bo De Chang- o A Ra Ba I Bo De O De Ma Sa

I Bo De A Ra Ba O So - I Bo De

Lead Singer(come sopra)

E - Kue Kue A Ro A Ma O Kue U Ra E

- Kue Kue A Ro A Ma O Kue U Ra E Kue Kue A Ro

A Ma O Kue A Kue Kue Kue A Ro E

- Kue Kue A Ro A Ma O Kue U Ra

Notes

Chapter One

1. Latin music historian Max Salazar states that the extensive use of the term "salsa" stems from the popularity of Cal Tjader's 1964 recording, *Soul Sauce.* In the recording, one clearly hears the phrase, "Salsa na ma." (Max Salazar, correspondence, September 1988).

2. Migene Gonzalez-Wippler, "Do You Remember the Cheetah?" *Latin NewYork*, Vol. VII, No. 4 (April, 1984), p. 29.

3. Birger Sulsbrück, Henrik Beck, and Karsten Simonsen, *Salsa Session*, Trans. Hugh Matthews (Copenhagen: Den Rytmiske Aftenskoles Forlag/Edition Wilhelm Hansen, 1988) p. 6.

4. Max Salazar, "History of Afro-Cuban Music," *Sonido Newsletter*, Vol. 1, no. 1 (May, 1981), p. 2. It is interesting that other words Latin musicians use to point out the "hotness" of a performance—"sabor" and "azucar" ("taste" and "sugar")—are also related to food.

5. Larry Birnbaum, "Tito Puente: Timbales' Titan," *Downbeat* Vol. 51, no. 1 (Jan. 1984), p. 61.

6. Roberta L. Singer, "Tradition and Innovation In Contemporary Latin Popular Music in New York City," *Latin American Music Review* Vol. 4, no. 2 (Fall/Winter 1983), p. 188.

7. Arnold Jay Smith, "Mongo Santamaria: Cuban King of the Congas," *Downbeat*, 21 April 1977, p. 20.

8. Cristobal Diaz Ayala, *Música Cubana del Areyto a la Nueva Trova* (San Juan: Editorial Cubanacan, 1981), p. 339.

9. Smith, "Mongo Santamaria," p. 20.

10. Sue Steward, "Daniel Ponce" Interview in *The Wire*, July 1985, p. 22

11. Salazar, "History of Afro-Cuban Music," p.4.

12. Max Salazar states that the first recording of a bugalú—a composition by Tony Pabon entitled "Pete's Boogaloo"—was made by the Pete Rodriguez Orchestra in 1966. (Max Salazar, personal interview, 1988.)

13. Roberta Singer and Robert Friedman, "Puerto Rican and Cuban Musical Expression in New York," p. 3. Liner notes to *Caliente =hot: Puerto Rican and Cuban Musical Expression in New York*, New World

Records NW244 (1977).

14. J. Emanuel Dufrasne Gonzalez, "La Homogeneidad de la Musica Caribena: Sobre la Música Comercial y Popular de Puerto Rico," Ph.D. dissertation, UCLA, 1985, p. 371.

15. Larry Birnbaum, "Puerto Rican Bands Dominate Salsa," *New York Times*, 4 January 1987, Section 2, p. 21–25.

16. Smith, "Mongo Santamaria," p. 20.

17. Migene Gonzalez-Wippler, "Do You Remember the Cheetah?" pp. 28–30.

18. Díaz Ayala, *Música Cubana del Areyto a la Nueva Trova*, p. 339.

Chapter Two

1. Fernando Ortiz, *La Clave Xilofonica de la Música Cubana* (Habana: Editorial Letras Cubanas, 1984. Originally published in 1935), p. 9.

2. John Santos, liner notes, *Music of Cuba*, Folkways Records FE 4064 (1985), p. 4.

3. John Miller Chernoff, *African Rhythm and African Sensibility: Aesthetics and Social Action in African Musical Idioms* (Chicago and London: University of Chicago, 1979), p. 50.

4. Birger Sulsbrück, Henrik Beck, and Karsten Simonsen, *Salsa Session*, Trans. Hugh Matthews (Copenhagen: Den Rytmiske Aftenskoles Forlag/Edition Wilhelm Hansen, 1988) p. 9.

5. Larry Birnbaum, "Tito Puente: Timbales' Titan," *Downbeat*, January 1984, p. 29.

Chapter Three

1. John Miller Chernoff, *African Rhythm and African Sensibility* (Chicago & London: University of Chicago, 1979), p. 51.

2. Roberta L. Singer, "Tradition and Innovation In Contemporary Latin Popular Music in New York City," *Latin American Music Review* 4 (Fall/Winter 1983), p. 195.

Chapter Four

1. Birger Sulsbrück, Henrik Beck, and Karsten Simonsen, *Salsa Session*, Trans. Hugh Matthews (Copenhagen: Den Rytmiske Aftenskoles Forlag/Edition Wilhelm Hansen, 1988) p. 35.

2. Argeliers Leon, "Notas para un Panorama de la Música Popular Cubana," *Revista Nacional de Cultura*, issue No. 204 (marzo), 1972, p.

51. See also: Sibyl Marcuse, *Musical Instruments: A Comprehensive Dictionary. New York*: W.W. Norton & Co., 1975), p. 443.

3. David Charles, *Conga, Bongo, and Timbale Techniques Live and In the Studio* (NewYork: Marimba Productions, 1982), p. 2.

4. John Santos, liner notes, *Music of Cuba* (Folkways FE 064, 1985), p. 1.

5. *Ibid.*, p. 2.

6. John Storm Roberts, *The Latin Linge: The Impact of Latin American Music on the United States* (New York: Oxford University Press, 1979), pp. 101–02.

7. *Cassell's Spanish Dictionary*, 1960 ed., s.v. "Tumbar."

8. Adela Lopez, "La Noche del Tumbao at the Garden," *Latin New York*, Vol. VII, no. 4, 1984, pp. 24–25.

9. For example, see Rhyna Moldes, *Folklorica Cubana: Con La Historia, Ritmos e Instrumentos de Origen Hispano-Africano* (Miami: Ediciones Universales, 1975), p. 39.

10. Humbertos Morales and Henry Adler, *How To Play Latin American Instruments* (Rockville Centre: Belwin, 1966), p. 10.

11. John Santos, liner notes, *The Cuban Danzón: Its Ancestors and Descendants*, Folkways FE 4066 (982).

12. Sulsbrück, Birger. *Latin-American Percussion: Rhythms and rhythm instruments from Cuba and Brazil*. Trans. Ethan Weisgard. Copenhagen: Den Rytmiske Aftenskoles Forlag/Edition Wilhelm Hansen, 1986.

13. Charles, *Conga, Bongo, and Timbale Techniques*, p. 5.

Chapter Five

1. Yoruba culture has had a profound and long-lasting effect on the Americas. See Robert Farris Thompson, *Flash of the Spirit: African and Afro-American Art and Philosophy* (New York: Vintage Books, 1984), Chapter 1.

2. The name "Lucumí" is still used in Africa for a Yoruba enclave in western Ibo country. See Darius L. Thieme, "A Descriptive Catalogue of Yoruba Musical Instruments" (Ph.D. dissertation, Catholic University, 1969), p. 187.

3. In 1960, a Detroit-born black who adopted the name Adefunmi founded the Yoruba Temple in Harlem. See Thompson, *Flash of the Spirit*, p. 90.

4. Fernando Ortiz, *Los Instrumentos de la Música Afrocubana*, 4 vols.

(Havana, 1954), vol. 4, p. 210.

5. Ortiz, *La Africanía de la Música Folklórica de Cuba* (Havana: Publicaciones del Ministerio de Educación, 1950), pp. 278–79.

6. *Ibid.*, pp. 280–81

7. *Ibid.*, p. 285.

Chapter Six

1. Felix Cortes, liner notes, *Totico y sus Rumberos*, Montuno MLP–515 (1981).

2. Birger Sulsbrück, *Latin-American Percussion: Rhythms and Rhythm Instruments from Cuba and Brazil*, trans. Ethan Weisgard (Copenhagen: Den Rytmiske Aftenskoles Forlag/Edition Wilhelm Hansen, 1986), p. 122.

3. Sáenz, Carmen Maria, "Música Tradicional de Cienfuegos," *Clave*, April, 1987, p. 7.

4. John Santos, liner notes, *Music of Cuba*, Folkways Records FE 4064 (1985), p. 2.

5. Cortes, liner notes, *Totico y sus Rumberos*.

6. Santos, liner notes, *Music of Cuba*, p. 2.

7. Pancho Cristal, liner notes, *Arsenio Rodriguez: Primitivo*, Roost AC210 (n.d.)

8. Peter Bloch, *La-Le-Lo-Lai: Puerto Rican Music and its Performers* (New York: Plus Ultra Educational Publishers, 1973), p. 23.

9. Cortes, liner notes, *Totico y sus Rumberos*, Montuno MLP–515 (1981).

10. John Storm Roberts, *Black Music of Two Worlds* (NY: Praeger, 1972), p. 96

11. Santos, liner notes, *Music of Cuba*, p. 2.

12. Argeliers Leon, "Notas para un Panorama de la Música Popular Cubana," *Revista Nacional de Cultura*, no. 204, (1972), p. 54.

13. The rumba ensemble consisting of three conga drums, claves and palitos was first augmented by bass and the tres (a Cuban guitar) in a 1950s recording by singer Totico (Eugenio Arango) and conguero "Patato" Valdez entitled *Patato y Totico*, RVC Records RVC 1102.

Chapter Seven

1. John Santos, liner notes, *The Cuban Danzón: Its Ancestors and Descendants*, Folkways Records FE 4066 (1982), p. 1.

2. Rhyna Moldes, *Música Folklórica Cubana: Con La Historia, Ritmos e In-*

*strumentos de Origen Hispano-African*o. (Miami: Ediciones Universales, 1975) p. 46.

3. Santos, liner notes, *The Cuban Danzón*, pp. 1–3.

4. *Ibid.*, p. 2.

5. John Storm Roberts, *The Latin Tinge: The Impact of Latin American Music on the United States* (New York: Oxford University Press, 1979), p. 8.

6. Santos, liner notes, *The Cuban Danzón*, p. 2.

7. *Ibid.*, p. 4.

8. Robert Farris Thompson, *Flash of the Spirit: African and Afro-American Art & Philosophy* (Vintage Books, 1984), pp. 110–11.

9. Santos, liner notes, The Cuban Danzó, pp. 2,5.

10. Arsenio Rodriguez is also credited with the development of the mambo. However, Max Salazar believes that Rodriguez' mambos, which at first were called "diablos" came afterwards, and were basically adaptations of Arcaño's new sound. (Max Salazar, correspondence, September 1988).

11. Max Salazar, "History of Afro-Cuban Music," *Sonido Newsletter*, May, 1981, p. 4.

12. Robert Farris Thompson, "Portrait of the Pachanga, The Music, The Players, The Dancers," *Caribe* 7, no. 1 & 2, p. 48.

13. Santos, liner notes, *The Cuban Danzón*, pp. 2, 5.

14. Salazar, Max, "History of Latin Music," Latin New York, November 1975, p. 30.

15. *Ibid.*

16. John Santos, liner notes, *Sexteto Habanero: La Historia del son Cubano (The Roots of Salsa, Vol. 2)*, Folklyric 9054 (n.d.).

17. J. Emanuel Dufrasne-Gonzalez, "La Homogeneidad de la Musica Caribena: Sobre la Musica Commercial y Popular de Puerto Rico," Ph.D. dissertation, UCLA, 1985, p. 432.

18. Santos, liner notes, *Sexteto Habanero*.

19. Cristobal Díaz Ayala, *Música Cubana del Areyto a la Nueva Trova* (San Juan: Editorial Cubanacan, 1981), p. 116–17.

G l o s s a r y

Abanico. Pick-up phrase played on the timbales.

Agrupación. See Son.

Amele. See Okónkolo.

Baqueteo. Timbales pattern popular before the 1950s. The baqueteo is a two measure pattern consisting of a steady stream of eighth notes played alternatively on various parts of the two timbales drums.

Batá. The principal and most important drums of Santería. Their rhythms are based on a drum language which reproduces the tonal changes and speech patterns of the Yoruba language.

Batalero. Batá player.

Bolero. Slow ballad in salsa.

Bomba. Afro-Puerto Rican genre; name for the drums performing bomba dances. It was adapted by Cortijo in the mid–1950s into a popular dance style, and has been taken up by salsa musicians.

Bombo. Bass drum played in comparsa; also, the second stroke of the clave.

Bongosero. Bongó player.

Botija. A clay jug tuned by filling it with varying amounts of water. The botija played the bass part in the early son groups; it was eventually replaced by the string bass.

Bugalú. Dance style based on the fusion of Afro-Cuban rhythms with the boogaloo, a rhythm popularized by Black Americans in the 1960s. The lyrics were sung in English.

Caja. See Iyá.

Capetillo. See Montuno.

Cáscara (lit. "rind, shell"). Two measure pattern played with two sticks ("palitos") on the side of the conga or on a woodblock in rumba, or on the sides of the timbales drums in a salsa group. Other names are gua-gua, catá and paila.

Catá. See Cáscara.

Cha cha chá. An offshoot of the mambo which uses a less-syncopated rhythm than the mambo. The cha cha chá often features unison singing by the members of the band and has a "sweet" rather than "hot" feeling. The name cha cha chá came from the sound produced by the dancers' sliding feet. Enrique Jorrín wrote the first cha cha chá in 1951.

Chaguoro. See Ichauoró.

Charanga (also charanga francesca, lit. "French military band"). An ensemble with roots in the early part of the 20th century consisting of the wooden Creole flute, piano, bass, violins, güiro and timbales.

Cinquillo. The characteristic rhythm of the danzón. In $^4_4$, it is a five-stroke figure which occupies one measure.

Cierre. Break figure, at the end of a section in a salsa arrangement.

Clave. Rhythmic formula which provides the foundation of salsa. The clave is a two measure pattern consisting of three strokes in the first measure and two strokes in the next. The clave pattern is most typically performed on the claves.

Comparsa. Cuban carnival music performed by a large battery of percussion and brass instruments. Marching along the streets, the musicians play the conga rhythm.

Conguero. Conga player.

Coro (lit. "chorus"). Passage sung by a chorus of back-up singers; section featuring the interplay between a lead singer and the coro. The coro section is also called the "montuno section," or simply "montuno."

Cruzao (shortened form of cruzado, lit. "crossed"). Adjective describing a phrase which sounds like it is played on the wrong measure of the clave—say, on the 3 part of the clave instead of the 2 part.

Cubop. Instrumental genre of the 1940s and early 1950s which was based on the fusion of bebop and Afro-Cuban music.

Danzón. Dance rhythm dating back to the last half of the nineteenth century which evolved from the French contradanse of the 18th century. It was performed by two ensembles: the orquesta típica and the charanga.

Diana. Opening section in some forms of rumba in which the lead singer sings vocables instead of words.

Décima. Poetic form used in various Afro-Cuban and Puerto Rican genres. The décima consists of ten-line verses in rhymed octosyllables. The rhyme scheme of the décima is as follows: first line with the fourth and fifth; the second line with the third; the sixth line with the seventh and tenth; the eighth with the ninth.

Descarga. Jam session format in the Latin music vein which was developed by Cuban musicians such as Cachao in the late 1950s.

Enú (Yoruba for "mouth"). The large head of each of the three batá drums.

Gallo. Name sometimes given to the lead singer in rumba.

Gua-gua (lit. "trivial thing"). See Cáscara.

Guaguancó. A form of rumba in a mid to fast tempo. The guaguancó is danced by a couple and pantomimes the man's efforts to seduce a woman and her repulsion of the man. If the man's efforts are successful, it climaxes in an act called "el vacunao." The text of the guaguancó deals with a commentary on everyday life.

Guía. Verse section of a salsa arrangement.

Guajeo. Repeated piano phrase, especially in the montuno section. English-speaking musicians sometimes use the term "vamp." Also, the repeated phrases played by violins in charangas. The term "montuneando" describes the process of playing guajeos.

Hembra (lit. "female"). Large head of the bongós. Also, lower pitched conga drum of a pair of conga drums. The other head is called "macho" ("male").

Ichauoró. String of small beads attached to the iyá. Also called chaguoro.

Inspiración. Any improvisation, especially a textual improvisation. English-speaking musicians use the term "inspiration."

Itotele. Middle drum in the batá ensemble.

Iyá (Yoruba for "mother"). The largest of the three drums in the batá ensemble. Also called caja.

Kónkolo. See Okónkolo.

Kpuátaki. Iyá player.

Lucumí. Cuban name for people of Yoruba descent.

Macho (lit. "male"). Small head of the bongós. Also, higher pitched conga drum of a pair of conga drums. The other head is called "hembra" ("female").

Mambo (Congolese word for "chant"). A dance style developed in the 1940s. "Mambo" was the name chosen by such different artists as Arcaño y sus Maravillas, Arsenio Rodriguez and Perez Prado to describe certain of the compositions they performed. Although the mambos of Arcaño, Arsenio Rodriguez and Perez Prado were different from each other, they shared at least one trait: the extensive use of guajeos, which served as a backdrop for instrumental solos and for polyphonic exchanges between one group of instruments and another.

—Also, the name of the instrumental section following the montuno in a salsa arrangement.

Marimbula. Large African-derived finger piano or sansa made of a series of metal tongues on a resonating box that are plucked. The marimbula was the bass of the early son groups; it was eventually replaced by the string bass.

Martillo (lit. "hammer"). The basic rhythm of the bongós.

Merengue. National dance of the Dominican Republic. The folkloric merengue is performed at a fast tempo by singers, accordion, the tambora drum and a metal scraper called a güira. (Note that the Cuban scraper is wooden, and is called a güiro.) In popular bands, the accordion is absent, and a piano is added to the rhythm section. The piano part in merengue bands is considerably fuller and "busier" than in salsa. Horns such as brass and or saxophones are present in the ensemble. Merengue arrangements use simple triadic harmonies rather than the jazz harmonies of salsa. The merengue is based on clave.

Montuneando. See Guajeo.

Moña. Instrumental section which follows the second coro section.

Montuno (lit. "rustic"). Section featuring the call and response interplay between the coro and a lead singer. Also, section featuring instrumental improvisations. The montuno is also called the coro section, or simply "coro." An obselete name is the capetillo.

Mozambique. Name given by Cuban bandleader Pello el Afrokán to his conga rhythm music of the early 1960s.

Ngoma. Bantu or Congolese drum ensemble played in Cuba; the forerunners of the conga drum family.

Okónkolo. Smallest of the three drums in the batá ensemble. Also called kónkolo, omele and amele.

Olubatá. Batá player.

Omele. See Okónkolo.

Orisha. Deity in the Santería religion.

Orquesta típica ("typical orchestra"). Cornet-led ensemble popular in the late 19th and early 20th centuries. The orquesta típica consisted of various woodwinds and brass instruments, a few strings, güiro and a pair of Creole kettle drums.

Paila. Timbales; also, see Cáscara.

Palitos ("little sticks"). Sticks played on a woodblock or any wooden surface such as the side of a conga drum; an accompanying part in rumba.

Palo. Congolese-derived religion practiced in Cuba.
—Also, alternate name for palitos.

Plena. Afro-Puerto Rican song form developed in the 1920s having a verse-refrain structure. The plena is often performed in an ensemble featuring the accordion; texts for the plena are topical in nature.

Quinto. Smallest conga drum.

Ritmo doble ("double time"). The final, mambo-like section of some arrangements of the cha cha chá.

Rumba. Afro-Cuban party music which incorporates percussion, dancing and commentary on everyday life. It is performed by an ensemble of three conga drums, palitos and claves with a lead singer and coro. Three forms of rumba performed today are the guaguancó, rumba columbia and yambú.

Rumba columbia. Rumba dance in a very fast $^6_8$. The rumba columbia is danced by a solo male dancer; the lyrics are usually in an African dialect such as Yoruba.

Rumbero. Musician who performs rumba.

Rumbón. Street performance of rumba.

Salsa (lit. "sauce"). Currently favored name for a form of music, formerly known simply as "Latin music," which has its roots in Cuban popular and folkloric music and is enhanced by jazz textures.

Santería. Yoruba-derived religion practiced primarily in Cuba, Puerto Rico and parts of the United States such as Miami and New York where there are large Cuban-American communities.

Segundo. Middle conga drum. Also called conga and tres golpes.

Sexteto. Son ensemble developed around 1920 which consisted of tres, guitar, string bass, bongós, maracas and claves. All the musicians sang except the bongosero.

Septeto. Same as the sexteto ensemble with a trumpet added.

Son. Ensemble based on a combination of guitars and percussion instruments, which developed in Oriente Province, the mountainous eastern-most part of Cuba, at the beginning of the 20th century. The son groups were also called agrupaciónes. The son compositions began with a short section called largo, in which the lyrics were pre-arranged, which was followed by a montuno.

Son conjunto. Ensemble developed in the 1930s to perform son compositions. Essentially it was the septeto instrumentation augmented by a piano and two more trumpets for a total of three.

Soneo. Improvised text of the lead singer (sonero) in a son group.

Sonero. Lead singer in a son group.

Songo. Cuban dance rhythm developed in the late 1960s which features a trap set performing timbales figures. Bongós are absent from the rhythm section. The conga player plays a busy-sounding variant of the guaguancó sequence of open tones rather than the tumbao.

Tambolero. Batá player.

Tcha tchá (Yoruba for "anus"). Small head of each of the three batá drums.

Timbalero. Timbales player.

Típica (lit. "typical"). Adjective used to describe music based on older sources, especially Cuban popular music of the 1940s.

Toque. Rhythmic pattern associated with a particular orisha in the Santería religion.

Tres. A guitar-like instrument of Cuban origin played with a plectrum. It is made up of three groups of doubled or tripled strings. Some tres players prefer to use guitars which have been converted into tres instruments by changing the chording and tuning.

Tresillo. Three-stroke figure derived from the cinquillo.

Tresista. Tres player.

Tumbadora. Largest of the three conga drums.

Tumbao (shortened form of tumbado, lit. "knocked down," etc.). Name given to the standard conga drum accompanying figure in salsa as well as the tumbadora part in rumba. Also, adjective describing a readily identifiable quality of a band.

Tumba. Conga drum.

Vacunao. Name given to a dance movement in some forms of rumba in which the man's seduction of his female partner is pantomimed. The vacunao comes from the Congolese fertility dance known as yuka.

Vasallo. Name sometimes given to the coro in rumba.

Yambú. Slow couple dance in $\frac{4}{4}$ featuring movements in imitation of the gait of old people. The yambú is performed on two packing crates with the accompaniment of a bottle struck by a coin.

Yoruba. Language of the Yoruba people of Nigeria; the ritual language of Santería.

An Annotated Bibliography and Discography

Bibliography

Traditional Afro-Cuban Music and Religious Beliefs

Friedman, Robert. "Making an Abstract World Concrete: Knowledge, Competence and Structural Dimensions of Performance Among Batá Drummers in Santería (Cuba, P.R., N.Y.)" Unpublished Ph.D. dissertation, Indiana University, 1982.

González-Wippler, Migene. *Santería: African Magic in Latin America.* New York: Original Products, 1981.

Moldes, Rhyna. *Música Folklórica Cubana: Con La Historia, Ritmos e Instrumentos de Origen Hispano-Africano.* Miami:Ediciones Universales, 1975.

Ortiz, Fernando. *Los Instrumentos de la Música Afrocubana.* Havana, 1954.

Sáenz, Carmen Maria "Música Tradicional de Cienfuegos," *Clave* 4, (April, 1987).

Thompson, Robert Farris. *Flash of the Spirit: African and Afro-American Art and Philosophy.* New York: Vintage Books, 1984.

Batá in Nigeria

Thieme, Darius L. "A Descriptive Catalogue of Yoruba Musical Instruments." Unpublished Ph.D. dissertation, Catholic University, 1969.

History of Latin Music Styles

Díaz Ayala, Cristobal. *Música Cubana del Areyto a la Nueva Trova.* San Juan: Editorial Cubanacan, 1981.

Leon, Argeliers. "Notas para un Panorama de la Música Popular Cubana," *Revista Nacional de Cultura*, issue no. 204 (marzo), 1972.

Roberts, John Storm. *The Latin Tinge: The Impact of Latin American Music on the United States.* New York: Oxford University Press, 1979.

Salazar, Max. "History of Afro-Cuban Music," *Sonido Newsletter*, Vol. 1, no. 1 (May, 1981).

Thompson, Robert Farris. "Portrait of the Pachanga, The Music, The Players, The Dancers," *Caribe* Vol. VII, No. 1 and 2, p. 48, reprinted from *The Saturday Review* (1961).

Latin Percussion Technique

Sulsbrück, Birger. *Latin-American Percussion: Rhythms and Rhythm Instruments from Cuba and Brazil.* Trans. Ethan Weisgard. Copenhagen: Den Rytmiske Aftenskoles Forlag/Edition Wilhelm Hansen,1986.

Discography

Many of the records listed in the discography are difficult to find; some are out of print. A well-known source of Latin records in New York is the Record Mart in the Times Square subway station. Recordings made in Cuba are available at the Record Mart and the Center for Cuban Studies. Records marked with an asterisk are listed in the Fall 1988 Schwann catalog.

Recordings with Liner Notes on Cuban Music

Caliente=hot: Puerto Rican and Cuban Musical Expression in New York, New World Records NW244 (1977).* Notes by Roberta Singer and Robert Friedman.

The Cuban Danzón: Its Ancestors and Descendants, Folkways FE 4066 (1982).* Notes by John Santos.

The Music of Cuba. Recorded by Verna Gillis in Cuba, 1978–79, Folkways FE 4064 (1985).* Notes by John Santos.

Sexteto Habanero. *La Historia de Son Cubano. The Roots of Salsa* Vol. II, Folklyric 9054. Notes by John Santos.

Totico y sus Rumberos, Montuno MLP–515 (1981). Notes by Felix Cortes.

Batá and Rumba

Guaguancó Matanzero, Conjunto/Los Papines. *Guaguancó*, Antilles Puchito LPD–565. The Conjunto Guaguancó Matanzero plays the Matanzas style of guaguancó; Los Papines is a show-biz oriented but excellent group.

Santamaria, Mongo. *Drums and Chants*, Tico LP 1149. Also has examples of nañigo cult music and the conga rhythm.

Totico y sus Rumberos. Montuno MLP–515 (1981). Contains an unusual performance of the rock 'n' roll classic "What's Your Name?"

Valdez, Carlos ("Patato"). *Ready for Freddy*, Latin Percussion Ventures LPV 419.

Valdez, Carlos ("Patato") and Totico. *Patato y Totico*, RVC 1102.

Bomba and Plena

Canario, Manuel Jimenez. *Plenas: Canario y su Groupo*, Ansonia ALP 1232.

Cortijo, Rafael y su Combo Original. *Juntos Otra Vez*, Coco CLP 113XX.

Early Son

Septeto Nacional de Ignacio Piñero. *Sones Cubanos*, Seeco SCLP–9278.

Sexteto Habanero. *La Historia de Son Cubano. The Roots of Salsa Vol. II*, Folklyric 9054.

Son Conjunto of the 1940s

Rodriguez, Arsenio. *Arsenio Rodriguez y su Conjunto*, Ansonia ALP 1337. Contains Rodriguez' song "Yambú en Serenata."

_____ *El Sentimiento de Arsenio*, Cariño DBM1–5802. Contains the palo ritual song "Dundunbanza" by Rodriguez.

La Sonora Matanzera. *Sings*, Stinson 92.*

Conjunto de Chapottin y sus Estrellas. *El Gran Chapottín*, Areito LD–3126 (EGREM, Cuba).

Big Band Latin Music of the 1950s

Prado, Perez. *Los Grandes Exitos de Perez Prado*, RCA
    International IL5–7293.*

Puente, Tito. *Dance Mania*, Cariño DBL 1–5017.

_____ Los Grandes Exitos de Tito Puente, RCA International
    IL5–7294 (1984).*

Machito and his Afro-Cuban Salseros. *Mucho Macho*, Pablo 2625714.

Rodriguez, Tito. *Hits*, WS–Latino WSLA 4060.

Descargas (Cuban-Style Jam Sessions)

Cachao y su Ritmo Caliente. *Cuban Jam Sessions in Miniature*,
    Panart 102–28037.

Alegre All-Stars, Vol. 4: *Way Out*, Alegre SLPA 8440.

Charanga

Arcaño y sus Maravillas. Areito LD–3917 (EGREM), Cuba. A recent
    recording of danzónes made famous by Arcaño's group in
    the 1940s.

Barretto, Ray. *Charanga Moderna*, Tico SLP 1087. Contains the 1962
    hit song "El Watusi."

Egües, Richard. *Sabrosona!* Siboney LD–341 (EGREM, Cuba).
    Contains the song "Se le ve" by Cachete Maldonado.

Fajardo, Jose. *Fajardo y sus Estrellas del 75*, Coco CLP 115XX.

Orquestra Aragon. Cariño DBL 5006.

Pacheco, Johnny. *Johnny Pacheco y su Charanga*, Alegre LPA 801;
    Alegre SLPA 8050.

Palmieri, Charlie. *Charanga Duboney: Echoes of an Era*, West Side
    Latino WS–LA–240–1.

Bugalú

Bataan, Joe. *Subway*, Fania LP 345.

Colon, Johnny. *Soul and Latin*, Cotique CS–1087.

Cuba, Joe. *Wanted Dead or Alive*, Tico SLP–1146. Contains the 1966 hit song, "Bang Bang."

Salsa

Barretto, Ray. *Indestructible*, Fania SLP 00456 (1973).

Blades, Ruben y Seis del Solar. *Agua de Luna*, Elektra Asylum 60721 (1987).* Blades' songs are loosely based on Gabriel Garcia Marquez' novel, *One Hundred Years of Solitude*. Piano playing and several arrangements by Oscar Hernández.

Carabalí. Primo RA418 (1988). Premiere recording of a new group under the direction of Oscar Hernández.

Colon, Willie. *The Good, The Bad, and the Ugly*, Fania LPS88460 (1975). Contains several arrangements by Marty Sheller.

La Conspiración. *Cado Loco Con su Tema*, Vaya XVS–29 Series 0598 (1974). With batá playing by John Amira.

Cruz, Celia and Johnny Pacheco. *Eternos*, Vaya JMVS–80 Series 0698.

Harlow, Larry. *El Judio Maravilloso*, Fania SLP 00490. Contains several compositions by Arsenio Rodriguez.

Libre. *Con Salsa . . . Con Ritmo–Vol. 1*, Salsoul SAL 4109.

Ortiz, Luis "Perico." *Entre Amigos*, Collectors Series (Ritmo Records and Perico Records) 8.98 Series. Contains several arrangements by Marty Sheller.

Pacheco, Johnny. *The Artist*, Fania LP 503. The music is in an updated son conjunto style; Frankie Malabe is the conga player.

Palmieri, Eddie. *The Sun of Latin Music*, Coco CLP 109XX.

Santamaria, Mongo. *El Bravo*, Caliente CLT–7074.

Sonora Ponceña. *Musical Conquest/Conquista Musical*, Inca SLP 1052 Series 0698 (1976). Contains the song "La Clave" by Joe Torres.

Songo

Batacumbele. *Con un Poco de Songo*, Tierrazo TLP 008 (1981). Contains an unusual danzón entitled "Danzaón."

Orquestra Ritmo Oriental. Areito LD–3622 (EGREM, Cuba 1978).

Los Van Van. *Al Son del Caribe*, Areito LD–4431 (EGREM, Cuba). Contains the song "Tierra Dura" by Ruben Blades.

Zaperoko. *Cosa de Locas*, Montuno 519 (1983). Contains an unusual composition entitled "Se Lo Que Es Rumba," which begins as a guaguancó and becomes a plena.

Afro-Cuban Jazz (also called Latin Jazz)

Dalto, Jorge and the Interamerican Band. *Oasis*, Concord Picante CJP–275 (1985).*

D'Rivera, Paquito. *Celebration*, Columbia FC–44077 (1988).*

Gillespie, Dizzy. *The Greatest of Dizzy Gillespie*, RCA LPM–2398 (M2PP–2019). Contains big band selections featuring conguero Chano Pozo.

Gonzalez, Jerry and the Fort Apache Band. *The River is Deep*, Enja 4040.* Contains traditional batá and rumba performances, and bebop compositions set to Latin rhythms such as the conga and the guaguancó.

Martinez, Sabu. *Jazz a l'Espagnole*, Alegre LPA 802 (early 1960s). Trumpet playing and arrangements by Marty Sheller.

Palmieri, Eddie. See Cal Tjader.

Puente, Tito and His Latin Jazz Ensemble. *Un Poco Loco*, Concord Picante CJP–329 (1987).*

Ruiz, Hilton. *Steppin' Into Beauty*, Steeplechace SCS–1158 (1987).*

Santamaria, Mongo. *Mongo at the Village Gate*, Battle BS96129 (1963). Trumpet playing by Marty Sheller.

Soloff, Lew. *Hanalei Bay*, Pro Jazz CDJ–601 (1986).* Contains the song "Salazar" by Marty Sheller.

Tjader, Cal. *Soul Sauce*, Verve 827756–1 (1986 reissue).*

Tjader, Cal and Eddie Palmieri. *El Sonido Nuevo: The New Soul Sound*, Verve V–8651 (1967). A good example of Eddie Palmieri's playing in the 1960s.

Indexes

Index of Names

Index of Subjects

 **YES!**

I would like to order the following White Cliffs publications from my local book or music store:

_____ *Salsa!: The Rhythm of Latin Music.* Charley Gerard with Marty Sheller. $39.95, hardcover. $14.95, paperback. $29.95, spiral. $12.95, accompanying audio cassette.

_____ *The Music of Santería: Traditional Rhythms of the Batá Drums.* John Amira and Steven Cornelius. $39.95, hardcover. $19.95, paperback. $29.95, spiral. $12.95, accompanying audio cassette.

_____ *The Drums of Vodou.* Lois Wilcken, featuring Frisner Augustin. $39.95, hardcover. $19.95, paperback. $29.95, spiral. $12.95, accompanying audio cassette.

_____ *Drum Damba: Talking Drum Lessons.* David Locke, featuring Abubakari Lunna. $39.95, hardcover. $17.95, paperback. $12.95, accompanying audio cassette. $59.95, Studio Perform ances Video. $59.95, Stories and Drummed Language Video

_____ *Drum Gahu: The Rhythms of West African Drumming.* David Locke. $39.95, hardcover. $15.95, paperback. $28.95, spiral. Set of three audio cassettes, correlated with book, $30.00.

_____ *Kpegisu: A War Drum of the Ewe.* David Locke, featuring Godwin Agbeli. $39.95, hardcover. $19.95, paperback. $12.95, accompanying audio cassette. $59.95, Studio Master Class Video. $79.95, Documentary Video filmed in Ghana by Godwin Agbeli.

_____ *Xylophone Music from Ghana.* Trevor Wiggins and Joseph Kobom. $12.95, paperback. $22.95, spiral. $12.95, audio cassette of performances by Joseph Kobom. $12.95, Examples audio cassette.

_____ *The New Folk Music.* Craig Harris. $19.95, paperback. Photos from the current folk, singer-songwriter and world music scene.

_____ *Synagogue Song in America.* Joseph A. Levine. $29.95, hardcover. $30.00, set of three accompanying audio cassettes.

The above titles are also available direct from the publisher.
Shipping and Handling: Add $2.50 for first item, .50 each additional, $5.00 maximum. Arizona residents add 6.5% sales tax. Overseas billed.

White Cliffs Media Company
P.O. Box 433, Tempe, AZ 85280 USA
Call 1-800-359-3210 for Visa, Mastercard, or Amex orders.